Pat,

Share the Wisdom!

Carol Seymour

# *wisdom* WARRIORS

## journeys through leadership AND life

### WOMEN WITH THE COURAGE TO BE TRUE TO THEMSELVES

## carol seymour

Signature
LEADERS
PRESS

ATLANTA

If you wish to contact Carol Seymour, please visit her website, www.signatureleaders.com.

Published by Signature Leaders Press, Atlanta, Georgia 30355

ISBN 978-0-9982615-6-0

Library of Congress Control Number: 2016918122

Printed in the United States of America

Design by Patricia Frey
Lotus design by Abby Pickus

First Edition

# Dedication

*For all the Wisdom Warriors who take the time to share a story and touch someone's life, and ultimately, make an incredible difference on their future. Leaving behind your stories and legacies change countless people for the better.*

*For my children:*
*To Rob, my son, my business partner, and, in the past year, my editor. I am in awe of your confident, savvy, and thoughtful approach to life's challenges, and ability to bring calm into our chaotic world. You are the strong foundation for family and growth, and I am so lucky (and delighted) to have you by my side.*

*To my daughter-in-law, Michelle. Your ability to stay true to yourself in a quiet, confident way and your courage to risk and grow give me the encouragement and hope that many like you will be the senior female leaders of our future.*

*To my daughter, Paige. There is no appropriate expression for the wonder of life and spiritual growth you have awakened in me and so many others. Giving of oneself for the service of others and sharing love with all walks of life are the most noble of all gifts.*

*To my new son-in law, Santos. Though we don't speak the same language, the power of respect, love, and grace is a universal conversation.*

*For my family:*
*To my deceased parents, Bob and Pokie Heisler. You are the original Wisdom Warriors. You believed I could be anything I wanted to be. I honor your legacies.*

*To my siblings, Yank, Sue, Nancie, Anita, Marsha, and Dede. Thank you for your unconditional love and support. Your circle of trust helps fill the gap in the absence of Bucko and Mimi.*

# Contents

# Foreword

## by Kathryn Beiser
Global Chair, Corporate Practice, Edelman

It's a beautiful fall evening in 2013, and I'm walking into another nondescript hotel ballroom. I can remember thinking I'd rather be sitting outside with friends than participating in a panel discussion.

But this particular panel was with C-suite level women executives as part of a Signature Leaders program, and I had a sense I might really enjoy the session. I knew they'd have substantive things to say about their careers and how they progressed through them, and I was hopeful that I'd be able to make a valuable contribution to the conversation.

When I walked in, I found the room buzzing with an incredible energy. In the audience were executive women from four continents who had spent the past 48 hours in intense introspection, examining their lives and careers in a way that was new and different ... and I could *feel* it. There was an unexpected intimacy with this group that had gathered.

The panel began, and I quickly realized my decades of experience were relevant. But what was so eye-opening to me was that these C-level women had gone through similar challenges in their careers as I had in mine, albeit in different environments, with different sorts of roles. Our shared experiences made me realize that there were more similarities than differences, and a whole lot more connectivity. I learned something valuable from each woman on the panel.

There were the questions from the participants, each more interesting than the last. The women who were in attendance, most of them on the cusp of C-suite as their next roles, had arrived with an eagerness to learn and grow, asking incredibly insightful questions. It was clear to me that the past two days had opened all sorts of doors that these women would soon walk through.

Looking back, a couple of moments stand out. It turned out that one of the attendees worked at my company and asked if I would mentor her. I believe that no one has all the answers, and mentors should get as much out of the relationship as the mentee, and so we worked together for about a year. It was a rewarding experience that I wouldn't have had otherwise.

I also found myself a bit envious that I hadn't had a similar experience earlier in my career. (Where was Signature Leaders then?) When things weren't going well and life got complicated, you just knuckled down, pushed through, and didn't complain. God forbid you admitted you had doubts, or didn't have all the answers. I know I would have benefited tremendously from hearing the stories of their experience and exchange of insight.

The good news (for me and for everyone else) is there's this wonderful new book, *Wisdom Warriors*.

Reading it brought me back to that nondescript ballroom. The profiles illuminate some of the same issues I've faced throughout my career and provide specific insights and guidance that will certainly help smooth the path for working women everywhere.

*Wisdom Warriors* champions being your most authentic self in the workplace. The gems I've taken from the executive profiles have helped me grow as a professional, but also as a human being. The idea that there's no one ideal path — well, that's an idea I wish I'd embraced earlier.

Nobody is perfect or has a perfect career. But if you're learning, growing, happy, and appreciated, that's the mark of a great career. *Wisdom Warriors* will help you define the terms of your own great career, and the words of these successful women will give you the strength to find your way.

—Kathryn Beiser
Global Chair, Corporate Practice | Edelman

# Introduction

It's early spring, and I'm camped in my adopted home in the western North Carolina mountains. There's lots of glass and light. I'm a big fan of this peaceful spot on a remote ridgeline. I've been writing since early morning, a blanket over my legs to combat the crisp air. By mid-afternoon, the sun is out and blazing. I take a salad outside and enjoy the view.

I'm trying to "take a page from my own book" (pun intended). Recovery time is key to our energy and clear thinking. But we need to constantly attend to it, create time for it. It's a commodity that quickly gets depleted.

As I eat, I recall a conversation with my daughter during one of our weekly calls. She is in Nicaragua, where she has spent the past few years helping lead a mission. "Take time out, Mom. Remember that doing nothing is *doing*."

I finally give in, close my eyes, and let my mind wander. So as I sit here doing nothing, nothing turns into a reflection of the conversations, the stories, and the excitement that all started in 2011.

✳ ✳ ✳

*I was having dinner with Roger Fransecky, a longtime coach to me and the rest of the senior team of World50.[1] Roger, who passed away in 2013, was a sage advisor to many large company CEOs, and we were fortunate to benefit from his ideas and suggestions. His time and words were gifts.*

*I was sharing a discussion that had transpired within our private membership group of top global human resources executives, a group I led at the time. Despite all of the work and attention placed on creating new programs for diversity and inclusion, these HR executives lamented that, despite a larger number of women in their companies, the needle hadn't moved on the number of women moving into the executive ranks. That sparked a discussion about what **would move the needle**, and I suggested creating a special program and network; a conversation **for women**, not about women, in a candid environment of learning, with special groups of peers. It would be a safe place to learn, ask questions, grow, and tap into one another, over time.*

*"Carol, I love this idea," Roger said. "Women are Wisdom Warriors. They know better than anyone how to pass along wisdom from mother to daughter, friend to friend, and colleague to colleague. Only, we don't do it enough in our business world."*

What started as a program has become an expedition. And now, after more than 1,000 interviews, and hundreds of executive women (and men) have joined in this journey, I reflect on how the opportunity to pass wisdom came to life. With each peer class of graduates, surrounded by C-suite leaders, CEOs, and members of company boards, the candid, safe, and open conversations happen. They are rich in wisdom, and, as a result, we all learn more. We hear practical approaches. We hear the same, simple things, often discussed in a new way — in a personal way. Everyone comes ready to learn. And we do.

At each of these sessions, I look around a room full of top-performing female executives, their eyes wide open, hands raised, poised to ask another question. And I see faces that want to soak up this knowledge: how to make life work amongst the demands of family and career; how to manage a tenuous boss relationship; how to stay true to oneself, while being asked to take a new role that wasn't part of the plan; and how to practice self-care, so we can be our best selves every day.

I realize more up-and-coming leaders should hear this wisdom. Each time we meet, I want 50 or 100 more women in the room to soak up the nuggets of wisdom we're exchanging. And as each program concludes, another group vows to pass the torch on to the women on their teams at the office and in their lives. It's great that so many women have benefited from The Signature Program. But there could be more, a lot more.

That's why I wrote this book. Sharing. Learning. Experiencing the lives and careers of other women, who are just like us. Maybe if we hear it in enough different ways, we'll take it in and incorporate their wisdom into our daily lives.

When I described this book to the many women who have been part of the expedition, they were excited. They didn't hesitate to raise their hands and say, "Count me in." But they often finished that sentence with something like, " ... though I'm not sure I have something to share that would be valuable." It didn't surprise me. That kind of comment stems from the same sort of thinking that has us saying out loud, "I'm fortunate to have this role."

It's not about fortune. It's about hard work, and experience. You might want a lot of things to happen in your professional life, but you're the only one who can put the steps in place to create the path. This book, these stories, will show you the way forward.

The stories in *Wisdom Warriors* are gathered from the executives who have attended, and taught, at The Signature Program over the years. They're candid and authentic about their experiences; honest about their missteps. We see them testing the waters, making mistakes, and sometimes failing. They show us vulnerability. On any given day, the ordinary of one's life might just be the story that changes another's.

Here's what I've learned: powerful women embrace every opportunity and take advantage of the possibilities. They *lead life intentionally*. That makes them better colleagues, mothers, spouses, friends, sisters, and leaders. It makes them better people.

How should you use this book? You could read it start to finish, or you can dive in when you feel a particular need.

✳ Struggling with finding some courage? Then flip to Chapter Two and check out some stories in the Power Up section.

✳ Do you have a colleague or direct report who needs some specific advice or direction? Grab a nugget of wisdom or answers on our Q&A pages to see how others approached the same issue.

✳ Do you want your daughter to benefit from the Warriors who preceded her? Put it on her bedside table, or wrap it as a birthday gift.

Or grab a glass of wine, sit by the hearth, and open the book to a random page. My hope is this patchwork of stories will inspire you in ways you had not envisioned before.

Whatever you do ... pass it along; to your neighbor, your direct report, your cousin, or your daughter. The torch of wisdom burns bright, and the Wisdom Warriors in this book share the honor of carrying it with you.

—Carol Seymour, January 2017

# Contributors

I am thankful to all of the contributors for sharing their stories among these pages. This book is but a small snippet of the thousands of stories and pages that could have been written. I am honored to be the recipient of their trust, and delighted to share their personal journeys of leadership AND life with you.

**Lucien Alziari,** Chief Human Resources Officer, Maersk Group

**Elsa Amouzgar,** VP – General Manager, Global Sales, ManpowerGroup

**Marcia J. Avedon, Ph.D.,** SVP, Human Resources, Communications and Corporate Affairs, Ingersoll Rand

**Patty Babler,** VP, NA Regional HR Solutions Lead, Cargill

**Kim Bailes,** Global Head of Loan Sales, ING Bank N.V.

**LeighAnne Baker,**\* Corporate SVP and Chief Human Resources Officer, Cargill

**Sarah Barron,** Global Head of Talent and Leadership, Arla Foods amba

**Joanne Bauer,**\* retired President, Health Care, Kimberly-Clark Corporation

**Sandra Beach Lin,**\* Board Member, American Electric Power, PolyOne, WESCO, and Interface Biologics

**Susan Beat,** former Managing Director, MUFG Union Bank, N.A.

**Kathryn Beiser,** Global Chair, Corporate Practice, Edelman

**Jewelle Bickford,**\* Partner, Evercore Wealth Management and Coalition Chair, Paradigm for Parity

**Maria Blasé,** President, HVAC and Transport – Latin America, Ingersoll Rand

**Devry Boughner Vorwerk,** Corporate VP, Global Corporate Affairs, Cargill

**Laura Brightwell,** former SVP, Public Affairs and Communications, Coca-Cola Enterprises, Inc.

**Katinka Bryson,** Agency Vice President, State Farm Insurance

**Lisa E. Butler,** VP, Strategy, MotionPoint

**Canda J. Carr,** VP, Global Channel Sales, TE Connectivity

**Katie Carter,** VP, Human Resources - Asia Pacific, Hyatt Hotels Corporation

**Jenny Cormack-Lendon,** Supply Chain Director, Cargill Agricultural Supply Chain, EMEA, Cargill

**Anda Cristescu,** Global Operations Director, Cargill Ocean Transportation, Cargill

**Que Thanh Dallara,** SVP, Corporate Strategy, TE Connectivity

**Catherine T. Doherty,** SVP and Group Executive, Clinical Franchise Solutions, Quest Diagnostics

**Kristie Dolan,** General Manager, Women's Health, Quest Diagnostics

**Ann Fandozzi,** CEO, ABRA Auto

**Julie Fasone Holder,**\* CEO and Founder, JFH Insights

**Kathy L. Fortmann,** President, Cargill Business Services, Cargill

**Frances Franken-Mulder,** General Manager, Gall & Gall B.V.

**Leticia Goncalves,** President – Europe and Middle East, Monsanto

**Andrea Grant,** Managing Director, People Ingenuity

**Kim Greene,** EVP and Chief Operating Officer, Southern Company

**Kari Groh,** VP, Communications, The Timken Company

**Veronica Hagen,**\* retired President and CEO, Polymer Group, Inc.

**Kristi Hedges,** Leadership Coach, Author, Speaker, The Hedges Company, LLC

**Cielo Hernandez,** VP, CFO of North America, Maersk Line

**Anne Hill,** SVP and Chief Human Resources Officer, Avery Dennison

**Susan Huppertz,** VP, Global Operations, TE Connectivity

**Deborah Jackson,**\* Founder and CEO, Plum Alley

**Sharon Johnson,** SVP, Quality, Product Development and Regulatory Affairs, Catalent, Inc.

**Tejal Karia,** VP, Financial Planning and Enterprise Risk Management, Catalent, Inc.

**Pam Kimmet,** Chief Human Resources Officer, Cardinal Health

**Linda Knoll,** Chief Human Resources Officer of CNH Industrial, N.V. and Chief Human Resources Officer of Fiat Chrysler Automobiles, N.V.

**Jane Leipold,** retired SVP, Human Resources, TE Connectivity

**Susan Liddie,** Group VP and Chief Information Officer, Avon Products, Inc.

**Sarena Lin,** President, Cargill Feed & Nutrition, Cargill

**Abbe Luersman,** Chief Human Resources Officer, Ahold Delhaize

**Sunita Mani,** former Executive, eBay

**Teri P. McClure,** Chief Human Resources Officer and SVP, Labor Relations, United Parcel Service of America, Inc.

**Heather A. Milligan,** SVP, Underwriting and New Business, Lincoln Financial Group

**Patti T. Milligan, MS, RD, CNS,** Partner and Director of Nutrition, Tignum

**Amanda Montgomery,** VP, Industrial Bearings, The Timken Company

**Elizabeth M. O'Brien,** Head of Enterprise Program Management Office, T. Rowe Price

**Ellie Patsalos,** Managing Director and Founder, Patsalos Consulting, Ltd.

**Leslie Pchola,** Area VP Operations S.E., Hilton Worldwide

**Scott Peltin,** Chief Performance Officer, Tignum

**Teresa Purtill,** Head of Customer Operations, Bord Gáis Energy

**Jeanne M. Quirk,** SVP, Mergers and Acquisitions, TE Connectivity

**Sonya McCullum Roberts,** President of Cargill Growth Ventures & Strategic Pricing, Cargill Protein, Cargill

**Rebecca Roes,** VP, Head of Accounting, Maersk Line

**Matt Schuyler,** Chief Human Resources Officer, Hilton Worldwide

**Maureen Sheehy,** former Managing Partner and Chair, Kilpatrick Townsend & Stockton

**Kim Skanson,** VP, Global Information Technology, Cargill

**Marilyn Skony Stamm,** CEO and Director, Stamm International Corp.

**Yvette Hill Smith,** General Manager, Global Customer Support Services – C&E, Microsoft

**Siobhan Smyth,** VP, Information Technology, Coca-Cola European Partners

**Hanne Søndergaard,** EVP and Chief Marketing Officer, Arla Foods amba

**Nese Tagma,** Managing Director, Global Edible Oil Solutions Europe, Cargill

**Cecile Thaxter,** General Manager, Newmont Mining Corporation

**Tina Tromiczak,** SVP, Global Business Solutions, ADP

**Eugenia Ulasewicz,** retired President Americas for Burberry and Non Executive Director for several public companies

**Karine Uzan-Mercie,** VP, Tax and Strategic Corporate Initiatives, Coca-Cola European Partners

**Kathleen Valentine,** General Manager, Prescription Drug Monitoring and Toxicology, Quest Diagnostics

**Annemieke van der Werff,** Chief Human Resources Officer for the Americas, MUFG Union Bank

**Joan Wainwright,** President, Channel and Customer Experience, TE Connectivity

**Robb Webb,** Chief Human Resources Officer, Tenet Healthcare Corporation

**Francesca Weissman,** SVP, Finance, Ahold USA

**Shanna Wendt,** VP, Communications, Coca-Cola European Partners

**Shereen Zarkani,** Global Head of Reefer Management, Maersk Line

*Denotes founding members of the Paradigm for Parity Coalition

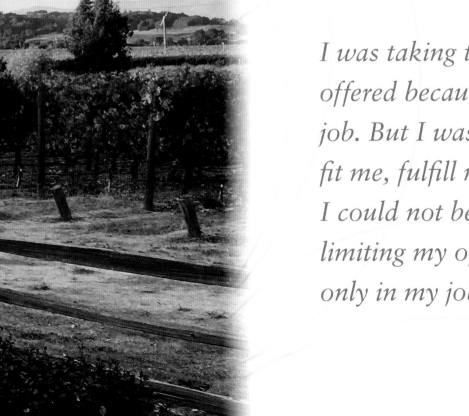

"Knowing yourself is the beginning of all wisdom."

— Aristotle

# Authenticity

*I was taking the opportunities that were offered because I felt lucky to have the job. But I was often in roles that didn't fit me, fulfill me, or make me happy. I could not be my best self, and it was limiting my opportunity for success, not only in my job, but in my life.*

# I started my career

in the decidedly unsexy paperboard industry, selling linerboard and corrugated box materials. I had to call on manufacturing plants in undesirable locations — not always the safest environment for a young lady wearing a skirt, blazer, and high heels. For seven years, I was the only female in the industry with this role.

I tried to fit in, but taking customers to lunch meant two martinis and a slew of dirty jokes. When I got back to the office, I often had to close my door and put my head on my desk for a nap. I had no female role models, so I emulated the leadership I saw — the command-and-control style, good old "tell" leaders. I actually did well. I opened a new office and a new market and grew significant revenue. I rapidly advanced and moved into new roles and, eventually, new companies.

In my mid-thirties on New Year's Eve, I took stock of my career, reflecting on where I had been. I realized that even though I was successful, I was not comfortable. The issue was not me, but the jobs I chose. They were just not the right fit for me.

My story is not unusual for women who started their careers in the late '70s. Many of the women in this book talk about wearing suits and floppy ties to fit into the man's world. The clothing conformity was not the problem. **We were compromising ourselves.** Fortunately, there are so many great examples of courage in this book from the same women leaders who dare to be authentic.

# And succeed BECAUSE of who they are.

## *Authenticity Shines Through*

In 2013, a friend suggested that I contact Ronee Hagen, CEO of Polymer Group, Inc. in Charlotte, North Carolina, to see if she would like to join our faculty at Signature Leaders. Ronee was the head of a $3.5 billion company owned by The Blackstone Private Equity Group. Ronee was the ONLY female CEO in their system consisting of more than 70 companies, and she was very successful. When I contacted her, she emailed me

---

Authentic means no difference between who you are at home and who you are at work. You are the same with friends and family as you are with colleagues.

Heather Milligan

SVP Underwriting and New Business | Lincoln Financial Group

# The Real Deal

We were looking for a head of marketing. I had a lot of candidates who came in and were trying to be what they thought a Chief Marketing Officer was supposed to look like. I wanted someone who was different. Someone who knew marketing, but who had an "on fire" mentality.

I met her at a hotel for breakfast in NYC. She was from New York, and **she *blew* in like there was a typhoon behind her. By my guess, she'd been out of the shower about 12 minutes. It was like a blur that screeched to a halt in front of me.** There's a hand. "It's really nice to meet you." I immediately thought, "I want to hire this woman. I love her. I love everything about her. I love the fact that she's spontaneous. She has to be authentic, because nobody would plan this."

We hired her as our head of marketing. She's amazing. She's a force of nature. That was because she was totally herself. It was a great first impression.

**Robb Webb**
**Chief Human Resources Officer | Tenet Healthcare Corporation**

back immediately, asking me to call her office to set up a phone call. When I did, Ronee answered the phone herself. **I was stunned. Never had I had a CEO answer his or her own phone!** When I mentioned it to her later, she started to laugh. "Well, that's because I learned long ago that it might be the most productive thing I get to do today." I'm not sure about that, but I do know for certain that she made me feel valued by answering my call. And I felt she was approachable. Calm. Delightful. Humorous. She was comfortable being herself — and a perfect example of authenticity. (You can read more about Ronee in her profile on the following page.) Ronee has since retired as an accomplished executive. She entered the workforce pre Title IX, and built a very successful track record, in part, because she refused to change who she was. *For anyone.*

Authenticity is one of the cornerstones of living one's signature. Leaders in this book are intentional about how they show up, who they are, and what their brand stands for.

## Becoming Your Authentic Self

There are several elements to authenticity. It starts with knowing yourself and understanding those unique gifts you bring. Add this to your core values and you can define your personal brand. Authenticity demands that you stay true to yourself no matter if your situation changes, your role changes, or you make a company change.

# Ronee Hagen

*Real life is what happens to all of us, and it's not nearly as perfect or as pretty as the written bios would have us think.*

My passion is to grow sustainable businesses to create better lives for families. That puts my feet on the floor every day.

**And for me, if it isn't sickness or death, nothing will rattle my cage. I can handle the rest of it.**

## Values-Based Decision Making

In every company I've run, we've always talked about values as the first thing. Values are the cultural glue that holds us together. When people know what their values are, decisions are easy.

Values aren't just rules on the wall; they come alive in the ways that we work together. And they remain the same every day.

*Ronee is the retired President and CEO of Polymer Group, Inc.*

Collaboration in a team, for instance, needs to be time based. When solving a problem, decide how much time you will spend, based on the information available at this point. Once a decision is made in the room, move on. When decisions are made in hallways, without process and integrity, the output will be suboptimal. There should be no hallway conversations, no pocket vetoes, no arguments outside the room. If you say you are going to do something, then go do it; don't leave the room and act differently. These are the rules that create openness.

**Have the courage to say, "This is the way we are going to think about this business." That's transferrable. And it gives people confidence. When people have the confidence to execute against the right vision, they will move mountains.**

## Play to Win

I believe it takes more courage to be a leader today than it did 40 years ago. It's much tougher. Whether you are running a domestic or an international business, your competition is now global. The intricacies of business, the time demands, the challenges ... there's a level of complexity in everyone's job that we didn't have in the past. Also, the expectation of speed and the need to respond quickly is there now. We have to make decisions with imperfect information and still have the courage to lead successfully.

In sports, there is a time limit to the game. In business, there is no buzzer marking the end of play. So what can easily happen? We play **not to lose**. Yet risk aversion is detrimental and disappointing. Have high expectations of yourself and your company.

**Business is a game you have to play and you have to play hard. The game is not going to be risk free. Playing not to lose is simply not enough.**

## Don't be Agreeable - be Memorable!

When you hire someone, you expect them to be very good at what they do. You expect they will be an excellent controller or HR leader. You will probably judge them on three things. Do they deliver results? Do they build great teams? Do they work well in a matrix?

When you are the one being hired, think about what it is that really makes you memorable and what makes you stand out at what you do. Identify your differentiator. Make sure others see it.

*Can you articulate why the company and the world are a better place because YOU sat in that chair?*

When you have a conversation with your supervisor, you need to be able to articulate how you created value for the company. Figure out metrics that show your direct involvement in value creation. If you are using company metrics such as, "We grew the gross profit in the company by 2%," then you are just mixing the metrics and spreading it like peanut butter. Speak *specifically* to your contribution to any and all parts of the business.

*If you think of yourself as the **owner** of the business, it really enhances your ability to drive value in **any** part of the business.*

# Be the Conductor

Moving from a functional role into running the business requires a different skill set. As GM or CEO, you've got to be the conductor of the symphony — not the best violinist. You have to really understand the whole orchestra and how it works, and be able to coordinate everyone playing together. Just because the violins aren't playing very well, you don't tell the tubas to play louder. That's what CEO-ism is all about.

# Knowing Yourself

Who are you? How are you valued? People often look at others to determine how they measure up. Andy Stanley, a Minister and Founder of North Point Ministries in Atlanta, points out that we all live in the land of "ER" — that place where we constantly measure our own self-worth against those around us. Our mind is cluttered with, "Is he smart**er**?" "Is she rich**er**?" "Is she pretti**er**?" We can always find someone else who has more "**er**."[1]

When I heard Andy speak, it was especially timely for me. I was in the midst of building a new business, and I had lots of advice from other people, which was terrific. But I also had many people asking if I had looked at this or that competitor to see how they approached things. Such comparisons were daunting — I constantly felt like I may be coming up short, and there's always one more competitor out there to look at. Before long, I was waking up every morning with a knot in my gut. So I decided to step back, calm down, and look back to my core, my signature. I remembered reading some William Faulkner during my college days and reflected on his encouragement to shoot higher than my own expectations and not compare myself to my contemporaries or predecessors.

With that in mind, I changed the measuring stick that I used for myself to that person in the mirror — "me." Comparing yourself to others can become a roadblock to knowing your authentic self. Instead, you should look inside at what makes you unique, and use those distinctions to your benefit.

## Perfectionism at its Worst

Another roadblock to understanding and appreciating yourself is the desire for perfection. The problem with perfectionism is that it can keep you from growing. Perfectionists don't like failure, so they avoid risk. They set the bar just high enough so that they are certain to achieve their goals, but no higher — which means they aren't stretching to discover new things and grow. It is important to get past perfectionism.

As Cielo Hernandez, VP and CFO of North America for Maersk Line, says,

"When I was younger, I would redo much of what my team presented to me because I wanted it to be perfect. This resulted in working what felt like 25 hours a day, which was not healthy, not productive, and had no value to my team at all. I had to learn how to be more accepting and appreciative of what others brought to the table. I discovered that coaching and mentoring is a far more useful and productive way to invest in developing my team. It is far more important to encourage the pursuit of excellence than to chastise for failure to achieve perfection."

## *We need to own who we are.*

In his book *Love Does*, Bob Goff tells a story about "Two Bunk John," a colleague working with him at a school in rural Uganda. John wanted to let two young men sleep in their office so that they could attend the school without having to walk 16 miles round trip every day. For a long time, Bob resisted. **He acted like many perfectionists do, aiming for small, achievable results instead of opening his mind to big, scary, possibly unattainable ideas**. But John eventually wore him down. Two turned into eight, and before long, they were running a large — and tremendously successful — boarding school housing 250 kids. Looking back on his original reluctance, Bob writes, "The problem with my plans is that they usually work. And if they don't seem to be working, I force them to work and I get the small results I aimed for. Swapping that for a big idea means you get everything that everyone brings" to the table.[2] If we allow perfectionism to limit the loftiness of our goals, we miss out on a greater opportunity to do amazing things.

There's another big reason why perfectionism is a problem. In reality, you just can't excel at everything. As you advance in your career and expand your scope of responsibilities, you have to pick the few areas you want to be known for. Frances Frei, Senior Associate Dean at Harvard Business School, has noted,[3] if you are to break out of the cycle of simply working harder and harder, "you do need enormous courage to say,

**'If I am going to be really good at something, I am going to be bad at something else.'"**

# Striving for Perfection Can Diminish our Leadership Effectiveness

---

*Many of us achieve our positions of leadership because of our attention to detail. In some cases, it can be driven by an overwhelming desire for perfectionism. It often results in micro-management to avoid mistakes. As my career progressed, I found I could no longer do everything to the final conclusive point. I think perhaps, one can only learn this lesson by experiencing massive failure on many fronts, all at the same time! This forced some self-reflection and assessment on what is important and how to lead an organization. I needed to experience the failure of perfectionism. There is also a people aspect to this lesson.*

**Being right, and having everybody know you are right, doesn't always end well.**

**Susan Huppertz**
VP Global Operations | TE Connectivity

# Ann Fandozzi

*When you have no road map, you have to chart your own course. Everything is possible, because you don't have a map of what not to do.*

My parents put their lives in jeopardy to leave communist Russia. Very few political refugees were granted permission, and we were one of the lucky ones. The three of us arrived in the US with two suitcases, as we had to leave everything behind. My father was 40 and did not speak any English, and neither did I. My mother had gone to the Conservatory in Russia, and she learned English there.

Starting a new life in the US was not easy, but my dad got an engineering job with Xerox and my mom taught piano. My only job was to go to school and do well. My parents would not let me do an afterschool job until I was a senior in high school. I relished that first waitressing job.

I was super geeky growing up and got a full scholarship to Stevens Institute of Technology in Hoboken by maintaining a certain GPA. Preparing for college, I took my first PSAT in the 10th grade and didn't do well (didn't break 1000!). I did not know anything about review courses before that test. My parents didn't know. We had no road map. There was no one to talk to.

My father moved us from state to state every time he got even a minor raise.

*Ann is the CEO of ABRA Auto*

**I was always the outsider. I never really fit in, so as a result I never tried to fit it. It's not a need I have because it's never been something that was possible for me. The good thing is, the need to fit in doesn't plague me.**

I would find it impossible to find parents that believe in somebody more than my parents believed in me. There are studies that correlate confidence to performance. "Believing you can" correlates to "being able to do."

## Success Enabled by the 0.0001%

I've always focused on talent and team. There is a percentage of people that are very successful in a particular environment. Let's call it 1% of the people. There is a much smaller percentage, call it the 0.0001%, that regardless of the circumstance, the situation, or the environment are still successful.

I spend an inordinate amount of my time looking for talent from the 0.0001%, spotting it, and nurturing it. Investing in them upfront, teaching them, including them in my thought process, and allowing them to grow through success and failure pays big dividends. I give and expect a lot, but if they can rise to the occasion, I reward them in a huge way.

As a result, I have created a network of talent that I would walk through fire for, and they would walk through fire for me. That is what creates capacity and followership, because no matter where I go, I have a Rolodex of people who are successful in any situation I need them for. These are people who when I pluck them from a situation, they will take a risk, and sometimes even a pay cut. I trust them implicitly. I speak to them in a shortcut. They know my expectations will be huge, and they don't want to let me down. **And I *never* let them down.**

How do I spot them? It's not easy. One is their thought process — how they approach a problem, how they verbalize it, how they attack it. Second is perseverance. When they fail, they pick themselves up. How quickly they do so and how they handle it is telling. How they ladder to that solution to find success is interesting to watch.

The ability to surround myself with incredible people increases my confidence and increases the ability to be successful.

## The Role of CEO

When a company is facing a huge amount of uncertainty, I believe the one thing that people need is a belief that there is a vision and a pillar of strength at the top.

**We may not know how we are going to get there, but I do know where we are headed. If people understand the course I am charting, even if it's an uncertain course, they can become part of the solution.**

It changes the conversation from, "We don't know the answer to the problem," to, "Let's figure it out together. Let's try A, let's try B, let's try C."

One of my least favorite quotes is, "It's business; it's not personal." I've never understood that because I spend so many hours doing it, that it feels very personal to me. I consider any growth company my baby, and that includes nurturing it and wanting it to succeed. That's probably been my biggest "a-ha" — I've had to pull back and say, "It actually is not my baby. I have 2 kids. They're my babies, and the company is a business." I feel very passionate about it, and I want it to succeed, but I have to be at an arm's length. If I'm too close, I'm not going to see things that, candidly, I need to see as the CEO.

The things I do at work are the things that I love. They are effectively my hobbies. Solving really difficult problems like a puzzle, figuring out the right answer, doing it with people I genuinely love and want to invest in — that's my passion and my energy. It just so happens to be the thing that I spend all day, every day, doing.

# Understanding Your Gifts

As you seek authenticity and stop measuring yourself against others, it makes sense to focus on your unique assets — your gifts. People often equate gifts with strengths, but the two are different. Strengths are those things that you are good at, that come inherently easily to you or that you do well because you have honed that skill over many years.

Your gifts are where you have energy and get energy. Imagine someone saying to you, "We have a new project, and we really want you to lead it because we know you're very good at this." Now you may in fact be very good at it, but what if the project itself doesn't excite you? Maybe it taps into skills you mastered a long time ago and, yes, you could do it, but it won't float your boat. You'd be bringing your strengths, but not your gifts, to the table.

Why is this important? **Because bringing your best self to any situation has significant impact for those around you.** When you are in your "gift zone," you bring enthusiasm and energy to the moment. People are drawn to your passion. They want to be around you, and you can give them energy — and that helps you engage and lead people.

## Finding My Own Gifts

When I started my career, I did not have a big plan. I actually couldn't have guessed what I would be doing today or imagined all the places I've been.

I knew enough about myself to have an idea of what would be a good combination. I learned along the way that I was actually good at Finance and in big business. I am fortunate to have worked — for more than 20 years — in some of the world's top companies in interesting and inspiring places, which were instrumental in shaping my professional career and outlook.

In my case it was OK not to have a big career plan. Developing my skills, enjoying my work, and keeping a sensitivity for business needs was key. Even now, at a more advanced stage of my career, **I find the closer I am to what I'm good at and what's important for the business, the more I enjoy my work and the more ready I am to see the opportunities, including those that may not be so obvious.**

**Rebecca Roes**
VP, Head of Accounting | Maersk Line

# Gift (noun)

## 1. The intersection of your strengths and your passion.

### What Are Your Gifts?

To find out, start with this simple exercise. Take a piece of paper and fold it down the middle so that you have a left column and a right column. Each evening, on the left side, record your highest energy moment of the day; the point where you felt like you were "on," driving value, and at your best. On the right side, put down that moment that drained your energy; when you felt like you were "off." Also, briefly record what you were doing in each moment. Were you presenting in a meeting? Interviewing a potential hire? Having a coaching session? Were you playing with your child?

Day 1
Presented new
marketing ideas to
executive team

Day 1
Sat in review
meeting on dress
code change

Day 2
Coached Hi-po on
building presence

Day 2
Created PowerPoint
for colleague

### Do You See Any Patterns?

After 30 days, go back through your notes to see if you can discover any patterns. Your highest energy moments are probably good indicators of what your gifts might be.

Armed with that knowledge, you can intentionally work to get more of those high-energy moments into your day, your week, and your life. You can also make a plan to get rid of the activities that are in the right column because those activities drain your energy and suck the joy out of life. **These energy suckers usually fall into one of three categories:**

- Something you've been doing for a long time that you don't really think about anymore and has somehow become just a habit (and which you may no longer need to do at all);
- Something that needs to be done, but which someone else in the organization could be doing (and which might give them a nice opportunity to develop); or
- Something you agreed to do because you were good at it, not because you were excited about it, but you felt you couldn't say no to.

*When I am in a role that fits my gift zone, I bring my A-game every day. In this moment, I am giving energy, I am engaged, my body language and facial expressions demonstrate passion, people want to be around me. These are the best leadership moments.*

By removing as many of those things on the right-hand side of your page as possible, you not only reduce their negative impact, but you create more space in your life to use more of your gifts.

Understanding your gifts helps you create a lens for making informed decisions about your life and your potential future roles. It helps you be intentional about your choices and stay on the right path as you move from role to role or city to city, or just through the stages of life. In my own experience, I was able to identify speed and growth as things that energized me. I now choose roles where I can use those qualities.

## Matching Skills, Passion, & Purpose

I think you have to make a match between what you do well and what the world needs. If you're passionate about what you're doing, because that's what you like doing, you're going to be successful. When someone comes into my office for an interview, and they have their eye on a job or on something specific, I always start with asking them about what do they really love doing. And often, it's not where they've been directing themselves. So I would say you start with your skills, and what really turns you on and makes you feel vital every day. Try to find a good match between that and a job. Then it's easy, because sometimes we get so busy that we're too busy to listen enough to hear. I think you have to give yourself some space and time to really listen to what's important to you.

### Joanne Bauer
**Retired President Health Care | Kimberly-Clark Corporation**

# The Power of Presence

When you are working in your "gift zone," you are able to bring energy and passion to your work that allows you to fully engage others. This is the first step toward incorporating the power of presence into our leadership capabilities. But what is presence?

When someone with presence comes into the room, you feel as if you are the only one they are talking to. People with presence use all of their body language; leaning in intently, taking in all that you have to say. Their eye contact shows you they are truly engaged and listening and care about what you are saying.

Good leaders have attributes that can be classified as hard skills, or competencies, such as expertise or knowledge in a given area, and soft skills, or connector skills, which include things like empathy, honesty, and listening. In her book, *The Power of Presence: Unlock Your Potential to Influence and Engage Others*, author Kristi Hedges suggests an exercise. Visualize the leader that you most admire. Then list five characteristics of their leadership that stand out. It is likely that at least four of the characteristics you named fall in the connector list.[4] Leaders with presence can connect with all kinds of people over many different kinds of situations. They have what some people call the "It" factor. And while it is hard to describe "It," you can see "It" in someone a mile away.

Former U.S. President Bill Clinton has this power of presence, and seeing him in action blew me away. When I was an executive at World50, we hosted an intimate gathering of 60 CEOs with Bill Clinton as the keynote speaker. When he finished his "stage" presentation, he walked off the stage and into the room. These CEOs were crowding around him in a large group, but with each and every person he met, his eyes and his focus were riveted on the individual in front of him. They knew he was giving them his total attention. His eyes never left that face in anticipation of the next conversation. That's presence.

Presence is not found in one's DNA. You can be a great communicator or have an engaging personality. But that does not mean you have presence. Presence is a skill that can be developed. And the nice thing about presence is that it requires you to bring your authentic self to the connection. Being who you are is the best way to show up.

Presence is a skill that often separates the memorable leaders from the competent leaders, but it is a skill that you have to also use at home with your family, the people you care about the most.

I heard a story about a father who always came home for dinner, but on one particular night, he was running late.

**He called his wife and asked that when he did get home, could he put the boys to bed before having dinner with her. When he arrived, he played with the boys, bathed the boys, and read them a story at bedtime. As he was preparing to turn out the lights, his youngest son said, *"Dad, can you come home late more often?"***

Being present is more important than "being around." No doubt this father was usually distracted by multiple demands when he got home, and this took away from his ability to focus on his children and be in that moment.

You can't be fully present if you are multi-tasking while interacting with someone. That's obvious in face-to-face meetings, but it's true on the phone and in conference calls, too. People on the line will feel it if you're checking emails while you talk. In one of our sessions, the women involved came up with two great tips to stay focused during virtual meetings:

- Get an accountability partner — someone who will sit in your office with you during the conference call. You can keep each other honest to give your full attention to the call.
- If you don't know the people on the other end of the line, print off their LinkedIn profiles and have them in front of you. It is much easier to engage when you know something about them and can visualize what they look like.

# Personal Brand

During a program, I once asked several executives,

**What is the difference between being a senior leader and being in the wings?**

## "That's easy. It's the Brand of You."

That was the statement made by Matt Schuyler, CHRO of Hilton Worldwide. He then shared with our Signature Program participants why he believes this.

When I was moving up the ranks at a professional services firm, I was up for partner. I flew overnight to London to receive my promotion, arriving at 10 a.m. My senior partner met me at Heathrow and said, "Matt, let's head to the pub." I thought this was normal, since it was London. When we sat down, he said, "Matt, I have good news and I have bad news. The bad news is you are not making partner this year." I was devastated! I had expected it, even told my family. Then he said, "The good news is you will make it next year IF you stop doing the things you are doing now and instead demonstrate your leadership brand. We know you already know how to do all this work. We don't want you to do the work; we want you to lead the work. People need to see who Matt Schuyler is as a leader.

# Q What is your Signature?

**Ann Fandozzi:** Fearless Geek. I'm not ashamed to admit that I love teeny-tiny numbers. It's fun for me and I like it, evidenced by when I was looking at the role that I have now, which is funded by a private equity firm.

They were telling me about the financial model of the business and it sounded too good to be true, so I said, "I would love to see some P&L statements." They sent me a PDF, like a screen grab. I said, "What is that? No, no, no, I want to see the Excel spreadsheets and ALL the details," and so the deal partner said, "I have never had a CEO ask that question." That's why I'm a geek, because I like little, tiny numbers, and fearless because I feel like when armed with enough information, you should not fear.

—Ann Fandozzi, CEO | ABRA Auto

**Joanne Bauer:** I am a catalyst for change. I love to move fast. I am constantly looking ahead to where we are going and never feel like we get there fast enough. I realized that while running a smaller division within a $20 billion company. Getting the opportunity to build something that was exciting and could change the face of the corporation was how I discovered I liked to be a change agent.

—Joanne Bauer, retired President Health Care | Kimberly-Clark Corporation

**Pam Kimmet:** Working in HR is so aligned with what I love to do as it allows me to impact individuals, teams, and the overall company in powerful ways; helping a person get the role they dreamed of, working through a problem, and helping a team be more effective. Seeing the massive difference that getting the right person in a senior leadership role can have on the company's trajectory is so incredibly rewarding. I believe in being business-focused, solutions-oriented, and proactive, but also always aim to be balanced and fair. Finally, I try to always conduct myself in a manner that conveys honesty and trust.

—Pam Kimmet, Chief Human Resources Officer | Cardinal Health

# Yvette Hill Smith

*I found that happy medium where I can be extremely professional but also be who I am.*

One of the best pieces of advice I've ever been given was to find a workplace and a business where I can feel comfortable being who I am. That's why I have always worked in environments where differences were valued and respected. That core value of respect for the employee is core to who and what I am.

As an African-American woman in corporate America, this has been about finding a level of authenticity that's comfortable, appropriate, and functional in the workplace. That advice had me really start to think about who I am. Who is this person who's a mother, a wife, a daughter, a 40-something woman, an African-American? How can I be me in a way that works for me and for my role?

**It has to work for me first, otherwise I can't be successful at my role or for my role.**

My family has an extremely hard work ethic. My grandfather worked at the post office. My dad was a world-renowned professor and he worked all the time, doing research and traveling. My mother always worked outside

*Yvette is the General Manager, Global Customer Support Services – C&E at Microsoft.*

the home, even when we were in school and she was getting her master's degree. I have their work ethic. Maybe that's why it's so important to me to bring my whole self to work.

I can't be one of those people who never talks about their kids or their husband or what they do in the evenings or on the weekend. I'm always working and these are part of who and what I am. I also have to be able to laugh at myself. I have to be able to be open with my mistakes. I have to be able to be in a bad mood and ask for forgiveness or, sometimes, give warnings.

**"Today is not the day. If you want a 'yes,' then save it for tomorrow."**

## Stumbling into a Turning Point

Ten years ago, I got a call from an organization in Toronto, Canada. I was in the basement of my church at the time, picking up the kids after school. Cellphone reception was bad, and I could hardly hear what they were saying. I was like, "Yeah, yeah, yeah. I can come up and help you." I didn't realize they were asking me to relocate. So a week later, when they called to tell me what the job assignment looked like, I said, "Wait, I thought I was just coming to help? I don't have the technical skills or the experience. I haven't been in this. I don't know how to do this, and I don't know how to do that." It wasn't until I got on site that I realized I had a really good set of experiences and skills that I could apply to the situation. Realizing that a great fit may not always look like a great fit until you arrive has served me well for every transition.

*Yvette*

## Building Your Personal Leadership Brand

Your self-awareness, your gifts, your presence — these are ingredients of your personal leadership brand. Your brand is the headline to describe who you are and how you want to be perceived. It is what people see and what you are known for. And if you live authentically, your words and actions will be in alignment.

You're probably more familiar with this concept than you might think. When someone planning a project says, **"We need someone just like Susan for this,"** there is an association with what a "Susan" stands for, delivers, does, says, and acts like. Susan has a brand that is recognized by others. It may be that people instantly recognize Susan as being open-minded and flexible. Maybe she is a go-getter. Maybe she is always positive and high energy. But the mention of her name among a group of people immediately creates a picture of Susan. If it's a positive picture, people will want to associate with her and advocate for her.

Your personal brand works just like a corporate brand. Every great brand in the marketplace evokes an emotional connection. Think of your favorite coffee shop. You can describe it in terms of its

# Brand is Critical, but Authenticity can be Hard

Seventy-nine percent of leaders believe brand is critical to their success but...

# 94%

admit to conforming to a culture or the "mold" of a role during their career.

*SOURCE: Survey of 60 Executives from The Signature Program*

signage, its location, its staff, its speed of service. All of these are facts. Now describe it in terms of how it makes you feel. I love Starbucks, and it is my favorite brand. I have a deep emotional connection with it. When I have a Starbucks triple shot, no foam, skim latte in my hand on a beautiful morning, I'm flying high. So I tell people about Starbucks — how great the lattes are, how the server had my coffee made when I walked in the door, how I crave their coffee, and how it makes me feel. That emotional attachment to this brand means I will go out of my way to advocate for it.

The same concept applies to people. Think of Germany's Chancellor, Angela Merkel. What would you say about her brand? She's the most powerful woman in the world. She's smart. She's tough. She's influential. And a lot of people in Germany call her Mutti, or mother of the nation. That's an emotional connection. **When people have an emotional connection with what makes you distinctive, they advocate for you.** That's what sponsorship is about in your company. You can't ask someone to be your sponsor. However, if you show your unique gifts and bring your A-game and energy to your interactions, advocacy is fairly easy.

A personal brand is not about puffing yourself up, listing accomplishments, or boasting. It's about building the reputation you want to have. When you create an effective personal brand, you have a consistent narrative for how you describe yourself — and a lens through which you can look at your actions to see if you are being true to yourself. In other words, your brand can provide guideposts that keep you centered.

# I Had Undervalued Myself

I interviewed for one of the biggest roles in my field a couple of years ago, and I still reflect on how poorly I performed in that interview. I honestly could squeal with shame thinking of the things I should have said and was quite capable of saying but didn't say.

That awful memory kept running in my head like a piece of software for a long time afterwards. But I know now it was a tangible example of how I had undervalued myself. Once I worked on my brand, began creating my narrative, and became able to articulate my leadership story, that software message changed completely. Now, my inner core conversation with myself is purposeful, positive, and intended to uncover the outcome I want to have, for every situation. Even for my year-end performance conversation, this mindset had me approach it in a very different way and opened up a more genuine conversation with my boss.

**Sarah Barron**
Global Head of Talent and Leadership | Arla Foods amba

# Defining My Own Story

My reputation was as a leader who looked after, and was accessible to her team. A former boss had once said to me before he went away to a European conference, "I need you to stay home and mind the house." I was happy to stay in the trenches. When I came into the program, I had tenure, long-standing credibility in my area, and a new promotion. But my brand was only strong inside the operation I was leading.

## I wasn't spending enough time creating a personal brand that was visible right across the organization.

Six weeks after I got back from The Signature Program, my boss and sponsor left the organization. He was the one who had opened doors for me and played a very strong role in helping forge my career. Three months later, our CHRO left, followed by our CFO, a business unit leader, and two other female leaders on our senior management team. Then the CEO left. We were left with an interim CHRO, an interim CEO, and a new CFO. Not only had my sponsors been decimated, the organization I was globally responsible for (customer care in the U.S., Europe, and Asia-Pacific) was one of the areas targeted for significant optimization. And we all know that significant optimization can mean a lot of things.

I found myself in the position of having to quickly draw upon the techniques I had learned at the program. I could not allow the length of time I had been with the company or my past achievements speak for me. I had to stay true to who I was at a time when the organization was going through a massive turnover in leadership. And I had to go out and project an image. I wondered to myself how I could do all that and secure my place in the restructuring. I thought,

## I'm not going to sit back and let something happen to me. I'm going to put myself out there on somebody's radar.

So within two weeks of the new CEO's arrival, I had crafted a note to him. I reinforced that my team and I were there to help drive the changes that were clearly needed in the company, that I was acutely aware that he and I had not yet had an opportunity to discuss our views on what my role would be, and that, appreciating the need to adapt, I would welcome a chance to sit and talk him through where I was going with my organization.

Teresa Purtill
Head of Customer Operations | Bord Gáis Energy

# Que Dallara

## *I know the source of my general impatience. It's why I work so hard.*

It's a very common story for any overseas Vietnamese.

I was born in Vietnam just a few years before the Vietnam War ended in 1975. My mother was a magistrate, and my father was in the South Vietnamese army. On the fall of Saigon, I was 3-ish. My father was sent to a concentration camp, and my mother was going to be sent in exile to a non-developed area. When you're on the losing side, they confiscate all of your property. My family was sent to a "New Economic Zone," a euphemism for a remote region without electricity or infrastructure. My parents decided to escape Vietnam, and on the third attempt, they did.

Thus, when I was 5, we were caught and spent time in jail. My father burnt our identity papers and claimed to be ethnically Chinese. As the Viet Cong had a policy of expelling ethnic Chinese, my parents, 3-year-old sister, and I were allowed to leave on a river cargo boat over the South China Sea.

As we traveled, the navy captured the ship, murdered the crew, and destroyed the navigation equipment so the boat was drifting helplessly for about a month until we were shipwrecked off a small island in the archipelago of the Philippines.

*Que is the SVP of Corporate Strategy of TE Connectivity*

## With no water or food for a long time, everyone, including the adults, were carried off the boat to the island.

After a month there, we ended up at a refugee camp in the Philippines. My mother, fluent in three languages, had written to the United Nations in French, asking for asylum and Luxembourg accepted our family. During this time, Australia's immigration policy changed and we were given asylum in that beautiful sunburnt country.

I did well in school and started a business when I was 16. With five employees and a turnover of $100,000 a year, it helped pay the bills and my university, and I was able to buy my mother a house.

### I had been running by 'Brute Force.'

Building the business was great experience to learn a range of skills from managing cash flow to leadership. After university, I joined McKinsey and had to sell the business. Having grown up in a working-class neighborhood, McKinsey was like a finishing school and had a big impact on my development.

While my hard work took me to a lot of opportunities, I feel I tried too much sometimes. You can overuse a strength, and sometimes you have to build the empathetic side and soft factors. I have had to work really hard to temper my impatience and allow people time for self-discovery.

I've always had a clear vision of the endgame I want to achieve and learn. I try to not let things distract me from that focus, and I work on the building blocks. It has allowed me to make changes quickly and has served me well in the role I now have as Chief Strategy Officer. I've really made a choice to focus on just a few critical things, and that makes life much easier. I've watched many people take on too many initiatives and yet fail to achieve breakthrough improvement. Leadership means creating the sense of purpose and providing some structure to get there. My intuition helps me focus on what really matters.

### You need to zero in on your priorities and have clarity on what is really important, because that enables you to move fast.

Some of the best counsel I've gotten is to take a new mindset in a new role. Try to forget the job you used to have and push yourself to do and get really good at the things you don't know.

I get my energy and contentment from my great husband, three little children, supportive family, and good friends. I have a personal life, and it is balanced and happy.

---

# Best Advice from Mom

Early on, my mom said, **If you get angry, you only hurt yourself because the person you are angry with doesn't know you are angry with them, so what is the point?** Her wisdom told me that being too emotional is just wasted time and can be destructive, especially if it leads you to lash out.

# Managing Perceptions

Identifying your brand is just one step. You also need to consciously shape how people perceive you, from the words you use to communicate your brand to the behaviors you show to demonstrate that brand. For example, when you are getting ready to give a presentation, your main focus is typically on the content and the questions that might be asked. But more importantly, you need to envision how you want to be perceived as you present, and what impression you want your audience to have when you are done.

## Aligning Words and Actions

In general, **actions speak louder than words** when you're building your personal brand.

You can tell people that you are dependable, but if you are always late to meetings, they won't use that word for you. Having said that, let's remember that the words matter, too. A recently promoted executive at a major financial services firm told me about her rocky start in her role overseeing strategy. "Every meeting, I was presenting the strategy, I was talking about the strategy," she says. "And two months into the job, I got feedback that I'm not very strategic. I wondered to myself, how can that be? So I went to a friend and asked what I was doing wrong. She said, 'You have to use the word strategy. You have to verbalize it and place it right in your presentations, and make sure it is on every page.' So that's what I did. And that shifted people's perceptions about me. *All it took was one little word.*"

## In short, you need to use both words *and* actions.

# Perception Is in the Eyes of the Beholder

Perception is the lens that people filter all information through. How someone perceives you — positively or negatively — heavily influences how they will interpret future behavior. Think of it for yourself. If someone walks into a room in a hurried way, and your perception of that person is that they're curt and abrupt, you're going to interpret this as rudeness. If your impression of that person is that they're energetic and efficient, you're going to interpret the behavior as busyness.

This is important work; understanding how you're perceived, and making sure your impression is aligned with your desired presence. **If you want to know how you're perceived, there's no better way than to ask.** I suggest using the question, "What's the general perception of me?" It's easier for people to answer as it generalizes the perspective and makes it less personal. This kind of feedback is invaluable and rare and can literally change your career trajectory. It brings to the surface issues you may not even have realized and can easily correct. I've seen this happen repeatedly.

## Kristi Hedges
### Leadership Coach, Author, and Speaker | The Hedges Company, LLC

**You communicate your brand through your narrative and execute your brand through your actions, and they need to be in alignment.**

Sometimes you need to think about how you are perceived before you even arrive. "A leadership guru once gave me great advice," recalls LeighAnne Baker, Corporate SVP and Chief Human Resources Officer for Cargill. "When you come into a room, stop at the door, throw your shoulders back, gaze straight ahead, and then walk in like you own the place. Don't slink in and go around to the back. Think to yourself, 'Everybody is here to see me. Everybody wants to spend time with me.' People will flock to you. I think it really works!"

Perception is a funny thing. How someone sees you is based on their experiences and preconceived filters. That means that you have to do "check-ins" with people to gauge their perceptions. You might not have the benefit that Kathy Fortmann had from an honest colleague who offered how she was being perceived without her asking.

## Pushed into the Nest

**I didn't know they thought about me like that!**

That's what went through my head when I was asked to take the Managing Partner role for my firm. It was a great boost of confidence to realize I was thought of in that way. I had led lots of litigation teams and had been very successful with that. But I had not been involved in firm management before and had joined the firm just three years earlier. I knew working with a lot of different people was a strength of mine. When you have an opportunity to do something that's going to expand your skills, give you some new outlets, and give you a different profile within the organization, you've got to take it. It was exciting, quite scary, and really invigorating. I feel like I have grown a ton from doing something that was a leap into the unknown.

**Maureen Sheehy**
Former Managing Partner and Chair |
Kilpatrick Townsend & Stockton LLP

## They Are Calling You the Ice Queen

Very early in my career, I was an engineer doing research for DuPont. Not only was I female amongst almost all men, I was much younger, as most of them were very senior chemists and engineers. I was worried about fitting in and being taken seriously. I caught on pretty quickly that if two women were talking, it was considered "gossip," whereas when two men were talking, it was networking, even if it was about sports. This observation impacted my behavior and I avoided hallway chit-chat.

One of my co-workers eventually had the courage to tell me, "They're calling you the ice queen." I was shocked and disappointed. He said, "I know you're not, but the perception you give ... ." I was so grateful that he pointed out I had been putting myself at an inherent disadvantage. I realized the thought I had not to chitchat meant I wasn't fitting in, and probably was why I felt more stressed, less fully in the content of meetings, and definitely not getting my best self across.

**Kathy Fortmann**
President, Cargill Business Services | Cargill

# Annemieke van der Werff

*Every exception you make, people will point a finger at you. But I never felt bad about being finger pointed. Sometimes you have to look at a situation and use another lens.*

I really like to unlock people's potential, but I also like to find things about me that I didn't know. I would never be able to work in a predictable job where every day is going to be the same.

I think that's why I love being in HR. Not a day goes by where something won't happen, with a person or with a group of people, that's never happened before and you have to find a solution. Recently we had a single parent pass away unexpectedly, leaving behind his young son. We

*Annemieke is the Chief Human Resources Officer for the Americas for MUFG Union Bank*

wanted to help, and at the same time, we have all kinds of policies established. It's easy to say, "We can't make exceptions."

This can be tricky business. What I like about that kind of situation is it forces you to think outside of your box.

**It forces you to be more resourceful. And it also forces you to look for pieces of yourself to add to the puzzle to make something happen.**

No matter what the situation, there's a lot of value in creating something that's going to help us all move forward. When these events occur, you don't resolve them just for the here and now. You think about what the effect could be. You think about the kind of person you want to be in this circumstance, and also the kind of company that you want to represent. That's what I like about the job that I do. There's so much richness when unfolding an issue.

I didn't start in HR. I actually started in banking, but I realized developing a team was more compelling than developing a portfolio of customers. When it came down to choosing this particular role and company, culture was a key factor in my final decision.

It's never just about the job and the people you're working with. It's also about the culture.

You cannot believe that the values described on corporate websites are actually the values people are living in the organization. That you can only distill from having profound conversations with more than just one person in the company and through exploring the actions they take. But before I spoke with anyone, I had a conversation with myself.

Am I still being challenged where I am now with what I'm trying to accomplish? If I cannot get something done where I am now, what is it? What am I missing here? Is it information? Or does the organization want something different than what I want? Is this company where I am now the place I want to be?

Then I got inquisitive. I raised key questions with people inside the other company.

What is this organization all about? Will it really give me the freedom that I need in how I operate in my function? How do you navigate in this industry? How do you navigate in this culture? How can you be part of it, help it and move it, rather than fight it?

**Authenticity is probably the most important anchor to hold onto. We've all been in places — whether that's in a role or a situation or even in a company — where that's more difficult. But that's where you have to *really* look at your true self and ask, "Does this feel alright?"**

*Annemieke*

## Later May Never Come

### The first "no" I heard in my career was the last time I actually listened to it.

I had a very clear idea about what I wanted to achieve in my work life. The bank I was working for had just merged and I knew there were plenty of opportunities. I basically walked in with a proposition of what I wanted to do. The answer was, "No, we have *this* in mind for you and *this* is where we see you going."

I remember walking out of that office thinking, "Later may never come. Later has to be now." Everybody may say it's the right thing for you to do. But some opportunities you really want to try and do. It has to be your decision and it has to feel right.

# The Courage to Stay the Course

Sometimes, staying true to your brand will require courage. In many cases, that may simply mean speaking up. The fact is, you may have the most brilliant idea in the room, but if no one can hear you, it won't have any impact.

Standing up to communicate and own your brand can take some courage, too. I remember Sunita Mani, an IT executive at eBay at the time, saying,

**"I had an allergic reaction to the idea of working on my personal brand. And then when we did the** work, it forced me to think about how I wanted to present myself. I realized that if I didn't own the impressions, someone else would. It made me get out of my comfort zone and manage my career so it wasn't just a wonderful accident."

A while ago, an executive called me to talk to me about a promotion she had been offered. It was good news, but she didn't sound truly excited to me, and I

## Don't Miss a Chance to Speak Up

Whenever you have an opportunity to speak up, you should. More often than not, you probably are sitting there, and someone else around that table has just given that idea, and you think, "Darn, I missed the opportunity to say that and it was on the tip of my tongue. I felt unsure." **Moving from management to true leadership and providing value across the enterprise requires you to find your voice.**

When I go to my executive leadership team meetings, my boss expects me not to only provide leadership on public affairs and communications, but he values what I have to say about other areas of the business. Whether we are discussing a commercial decision to change our cap size or if we want to lower sugar content in a package or how we want to interact with the customers, he is looking for my input. Is that really my wheelhouse of expertise? No, but he values my input as someone on the leadership team.

**Laura Brightwell**
Former SVP, Public Affairs and Communications | Coca-Cola Enterprises, Inc.

told her so. She admitted, "Well, frankly, I've really reflected on who I am and what I'm passionate about, and **I don't think this is the best opportunity for me. Can I do it? Yes. Do they know I can do it? Yes. But I don't think it's the thing that is going to drive me every day and get me excited. So I'm going to turn it down."**

## *And she did.*

Three months later, she called again to tell me about another opportunity — again, not a great fit. "But now I'm afraid that turning it down will be political suicide," she said. So I asked her what she wanted to do. "I'm really passionate about innovation," she said. "That's what lights my fire." I asked who had that role in the company now, and she answered, "No one." So I suggested that she go back and have a conversation about the value she could bring the company in that area, and drive the conversation to create a role for herself. The company ended up having her lead this effort — with the title, Head of Innovation — to add to her existing role. She didn't mind, because it gave her the white space and the energy to bring her best to the company. Her excitement and passion showed through, she engaged more people, and she was seen as a better leader. And within six months, she called me again to say she'd just been promoted to a position on the executive committee.

# Can You Hear Me?

*Many women have voices that just aren't heard. They can't seem to get their message across. I think part of it is bias, part of it physical. You have to cross both bridges.*

*Picture your house burning down. When the fire department arrives, the first firefighter you see is a 120-pound woman. You're thinking, "Where's the big guy who's really going to take care of the fire?" That firefighter has a brief window of time to bridge that mental bubble coming out of your head that's saying, "Maybe this is not the right person to do the job." It can be a short bridge or a long one. It can be very steep or it can be a pretty flat, easy go. But you have to build it. Don't fight it.*

**Acknowledge it and figure out what you have that might create that bridge.**

**Ronee Hagen**
Retired President & CEO | Polymer Group, Inc.

# Jewelle Bickford

*If you're not happy and it's not absolutely the highest and best use of your skills, I don't think you'll ever achieve what you could achieve.*

My father was an entrepreneur who chased deals — what we used to call a promoter and what we now call an investment banker. He was exceedingly good at it. In the early years, he was *very* successful. He was always chasing the dollar. But his values were almost as bad as his skills were good.

By the time I was 20, we had lived in nine places. He had lost all his money with too many women, too many deals, too many this and that. The kids fell between the cracks. I learned what I *didn't* want.

**In our family, my father had the power. My mother was powerless. As a young child, I learned I did not want to be powerless.**

I decided I would create the home I never had. I was going to marry someone who was stable and loving and who wanted a home and family as much as I did. I picked the right man and designed my life from there to have the right balance.

In 1980, when I was fired from Citibank, I went to the head of outplacements. He gave me a battery of tests. He said I scored 99.3 on the percentile for

*Jewelle is a Partner of Evercore Wealth Management and the Coalition Chair for Paradigm for Parity*

# The Power in Pacing

If you think you know the right answer, like a child, you want your hand up in the air. "Here, yes, yes, call on me because I know!" That can be exceedingly annoying to other people. And being a woman (and often the only woman at the table at that time), whatever I said could be dismissed more easily. The best advice came from a man that fired me. He suggested I could be more effective if I waited.

*I had to go slower, listen more, and not always offer my opinion right out of the gate.*

investment banking and that it was very clear that I would do well in that business.

I had my father's skills and the same sort of ability to see the angles, to see the opportunities, to see the possibilities. I became one of the very few women at that time in that field. As the years went on, I became proud I had those skills. And I realized with some compassion how much my father had been shaped by his upbringing and environment, just as I had been. It didn't occur to me that, besides what I didn't want, I had learned a great deal from watching my father that was positive.

When I was going through my mother's things after her death, I found all my school records. One of my professors had written, "Your daughter is *naturally disputatious*." My mother had thought that was the worst thing in the world, to be always arguing. I didn't look at it as arguing. I looked at it as asking questions. I questioned assumptions. I believed then, as I do now, that is very healthy. It allows you to see things others don't, it keeps you out of trouble, and often it puts you on the right track in both your personal and professional life.

## I never tried to fit myself into a pattern, a company, or a business where I didn't fit.

So many people do something because they're well paid or they think they will be well paid. I found the right fit by making a match between what I do well — or what I could do well — and what the world wants and will pay for. That has contributed to my success and happiness after my

retirement from investment banking. More opportunities to use my skills appeared after I "officially" retired. GenSpring opened the door to working as a senior strategist with high net worth families. My interest in women and their relationship to wealth led me to the investment advisory firm, Evercore, where I am a Partner, and allowed my involvement with the Paradigm for Parity℠ movement.

## Women are often so busy trying to do it all that they don't take care of the things that are most important in their lives. Sometimes this is their health. Often it is their finances.

I have so many women who come into my office at Evercore now saying, "I didn't put as much in my 401(k) as I should have," or "I didn't exercise these stock options because I was so busy," or "I never thought about separating my money and now I'm getting a divorce." Just because you can read a balance sheet doesn't mean you know anything about investing your money. I have experienced the entire arc of a woman's life. That helps me guide women and their families towards the different products that have different roles at different phases in their financial life cycle.

*Jewelle*

# Embracing Your Vulnerability

Courage to stay true to your brand allows you to remain authentic in tough situations. Equally as important is the ability to share your imperfections and your insecurities, which also helps you to be your authentic self. Of course, vulnerability is typically considered a sign of weakness — and leaders are supposed to be strong, right? So, women often work hard to avoid being seen as vulnerable. As a result, women don't talk about their lives while at work — their families, their problems, their joys.

You may try to hide that there are things that you might not know about a project or the business.

In reality, vulnerability is not a weakness. It's an asset. When you tell people you don't know, when you let them into your life, you become more human, more approachable.

---

## It's Tough to Ask for Help

I used to think the word vulnerability was very much a handicap in the workplace. I often felt that bringing your A-game meant you had to be poker-faced, and all in; no emotion. For me, it took a crisis situation for that to change. My daughter had a lot of health issues; she needed heart surgery years ago, and I had just been promoted to a VP position. It's very difficult when you have major things going on in your life and you're in a new leadership role. You realize people are more uncomfortable to actually talk to you. They see you by your title, and not as the person you are. I was at a point in my life where I couldn't separate my home life with work; I had to ask people for help and lean on my team. That was hard to ask. What I realized was that when you show vulnerability, people like to help.

People feel valued and empowered when you ask them to step in for you. I always made work about work.

**In reality, it's the person that shows up ... that's what your team wants to see.**

### Fran Weissman
SVP, Finance | Ahold USA

## The Courage to be Confidently Vulnerable

What do I mean? Show your outward confidence. I learned over the years that having confidence doesn't mean that you've got to be right all the time. The more senior you become, the more you realize there's a lot you don't know. In reality, it takes courage to tell people, "I don't know this. *You* might be the best person to answer it. Come and help me learn. Let's figure out the best solution." It takes courage to say, "I don't know," but you've got to say it in a confident way. That's why I say you have to have the courage to be confidently vulnerable.

### Sarena Lin
President, Cargill Feed & Nutrition | Cargill

# Q Can you be authentic and stay true to yourself?

**Ann Fandozzi:** Not only can you, I think you need to. You owe it to yourself, and to your organization, to be true to yourself. People feel authenticity. They even feel it in emails. Being true to yourself may be a bit overwhelming. If that is really who you are and the culture doesn't allow that, the doors are closed. Period. But if that culture is forcing you to be someone different, don't you owe it to yourself to be authentic? Even if it means ultimately walking away.

—Ann Fandozzi, CEO | ABRA Auto

**Joanne Bauer:** I believe you can be authentic and stay true to your brand. First of all, trust is huge. I led a pretty big cultural change that we started in my division, which was later adopted by the company. It was all around feedback and open communication with people. I think that standing in front of people, and really helping them understand what the vision is and your commitment to it, and then listening to their feedback and acting on it, can make you very authentic.

—Joanne Bauer, retired President Health Care | Kimberly-Clark Corporation

**Maureen Sheehy:** I have gotten as far as I have because of my authenticity. You have to recognize there are people who would have you be something different because that's who they are. Remaining true to what resounds with you is what gets you there. It's about trusting your instincts.

—Maureen Sheehy, former Managing Partner and Chair | Kilpatrick Townsend & Stockton

**Sandra Beach Lin:** I really play to my strengths as much as possible, and I don't ignore my own developmental needs. I am detail-oriented, yet I am also strategic. One of my colleagues remarked, "You know, all the board members know that you're really prepared and it's upped their game." That's authentic for me. I didn't have to change who I am.

—Sandra Beach Lin, Board Member | American Electric Power, PolyOne, WESCO, and Interface Biologics

# LeighAnne Baker

## *I didn't change what I am. I am what I am. What I changed was my mindset around what was holding me back.*

For a long time, I believed I was just so lucky to be in business at all. It never occurred to me that I could be in the number-one HR job in the C-suite. Having come from small-town Ohio, corporate executives were just not part of my world. I was glad to go to college and study mathematics, land some great jobs, be the high-potential team player that everyone wanted on their team. I was very happy to be a strong number two.

**My belief that I was just lucky to be where I was really held me back. It wasn't until I became confident enough to say, "I'm lucky, and I've worked damn hard to get here!" that I could acknowledge to myself that I really wanted to be a Chief HR Officer.**

## You Have to Ask!

The company that hired me after college understood I wanted to be a plant manager. I kept going to more roles because I thought that was what I needed to be plant manager. I thought all my hard

*LeighAnne is the Corporate SVP, Chief Human Resources Officer of Cargill*

work would pay off, but others kept getting the open plant manager jobs. It took me a while to figure it out. Finally I asked the vice president directly, "What else do I need to do? When are you going to let me run a plant?" *I was that bold.* The next plant opening was mine. I walked into a pile of trouble, but I got the job.

That first week, we received a petition across the fax saying that the plant workers wanted to organize with a strong union. This problem was all mine to fix. I thought, "I've done all this work to get here and now I might be fired." That was my first "oh, sh∗t" moment. But the experience ended up changing my career. We convinced the employees to stay non-union. While this was happening, I made frequent presentations to the chairman of the board on what we were doing. That got me noticed, and the company ended up sending me to Stanford Business School. Going to Stanford gave me the confidence to realize I really could be a CHRO. Years later, in spite of how much I liked my company, I chose to leave. I had been hanging at the level below the top job, and I realized it would be several years more before the number-one job opened up there. It was time for me to move on.

I need constant growth and intellectual stimulation. I need to feel I can make an impact and push an organization forward. I'm not afraid of being fired, so I'm willing to push.

## It's not that I work less hours; it's that I am managing what I choose to work on.

As a CHRO, the main things you do include succession planning, managing your team, looking at the longer-term view of talent for the company. These, plus working with the board. I passionately love what we are doing and do not think of it as work. It is what drives me every day.

## Go where the opportunities are and be willing to take risks. That may mean that when you get to the fork in the road, you take the path that's less traveled.

I thought I may negatively impact my children's lives with my many moves throughout my career. My daughter ended up going to three different high schools. When it was time for her to do her college entrance exam, she came to me and said, "I know what I'm going to write about. I'm going to write about how you made me move as I was growing up." I thought, "Oh, my God, she's going to need a therapist by the time this is done." Wise beyond her years, she wrote the most positive college essay about how moving for her mom's career helped her grow as a person. Now I think of those moves as opportunities I gave them to do all these wonderful things. My kids, who are now young adults, are fearless. They know how to navigate an airport with the best of them.

*LeighAnne*

# Resilience

## Expect criticism when you take on a senior leadership role in the C-suite.

*When negative things are happening outside your control, you can say, "Woe is me," and be the victim. Or you can be resilient and accept that this is what you have, look that reality in the face, roll up your sleeves, and deal with it.*

*If you are pushing the organization forward, you will have critics. If you're just managing the status quo or trying to be liked by everyone, then you won't have critics, but you also won't have impact. You have to have thick skin. You have to have conviction that you're doing the right thing for the overall organization and the courage to just keep pushing.*

# Why Don't You Smile Anymore?

**I don't typically share the personal side of myself at work, but I felt really good doing so.** And it changed the way people see me in a positive way.

I didn't realize I was becoming more intense at work, day to day, running non-stop, 70 miles an hour, until a colleague of mine stopped me in the hall as we were passing, and said, "You know, Kathleen, you don't smile anymore. You always used to smile, but you don't smile anymore." It felt like a punch in the gut. I was letting myself get caught up in work, and I didn't realize how I was showing myself to others. That happened right before I came to the program.

A few months later, my company asked me to come to a breakfast series they planned so employees would have a chance to get to know their leaders more informally. The idea was to speak about myself in whatever way I wanted for a few minutes, then open it up to a Q&A.

My style at work is "get my job done and get out." I don't do a lot of chit-chatting, asking others how their kids are doing or "how was the soccer game?" So for a heads-down, let's-get-it-done kind of person like me, this was a great opportunity to tell people who I am in a more casual setting.

I recalled being at The Signature Program and how impressed I was with CEO Ronee Hagen's presentation, which was one slide of just her family photo — the basis of her values and decision making. She was so approachable and authentic.

I consciously decided to go to this breakfast and bring a few of my own family photos. **It was a very vulnerable five minutes.** I put up one photo of my family, explaining how vitally important they are to me, and then shared a story of my sons when they were very young.

People loved the story, and a few came up afterward and said, "I had no idea you had three boys!" Sharing myself in this way changed the way they looked at me.

Kathleen Valentine
General Manager, Prescription Drug Monitoring & Toxicology | Quest Diagnostics

# Making Sure You FIT

During your career, you may find yourself in a working environment that has an edge of stress related to it that you can't explain. When I had my post-session call with an SVP from a top retailer, she shared an observation that really stood out. She said, "I realized, as I listened to the women in our network, that my situation might have been more unique, in that I worked in an organization where women were the majority, not the minority. We had a female CEO, too.

"I never thought about doing anything other than going into work and focusing on the problems I needed to solve, whereas many of the women in the network first had to think about fitting in to their environment before they even had a chance to start their work. That has to be draining on their mind-share and ability to bring energy."

Fit is one of the most undervalued contributors of leadership success in an organization. If you are constantly fighting inside your gut on how you need to approach a situation or how you are being perceived, the energy spent outweighs your ability to be truly effective. The Wisdom Warriors in this book are very vocal to advise other women to find the right environment where their gifts can be utilized and where they can drive the greatest contribution. When you walk into your office, if the stress that hits you is associated with how you fit in the culture, you are wasting too many brain cells.

**Feeling like you fit makes you more comfortable, and when that happens, you make other people feel more comfortable.**

*"I found that I needed to have a much stronger personal statement. It needs to identify, and very clearly state, the two or three things for which I am known and valued in my company; the things that help me make more contributions to my company. I have highlighted this personal statement on my LinkedIn profile."*

Tejal Karia, VP Tax and Enterprise Risk Management | Catalent, Inc.

# Katinka Bryson

## Spending time with people gives you a leadership opportunity

As a young girl, I believed that there was no limit to what I could get done or to what I would be willing to take on. I felt my father's pleasure in this, and I was heavily rewarded and stroked for my approach to tasks, events, and life. This kind of approach is what my college professor described as a "checklist mentality," which is basically the ambition or determination to do as much as possible in one day.

Early in my career, my checklist mentality was off the charts. I didn't set out to intentionally value my career more than those I was working with, but there is something intoxicating and rewarding about succeeding at the checklist game. This was an individual sport and I knew I could win!

*Katinka is the Agency VP of State Farm Insurance*

However, I found that this limited my ability to connect with people and build relationships. Most importantly, it limited my effectiveness as a leader. Today, I am intentional about how and where I meet with others.

### Rise Above The Fray, But Do It With Grace

Years ago, when I was a fairly new vice president, I received the best coaching from my boss that has helped me time and again. At the time, I had three peers, and I was the youngest and newest to the role by a number of years. There seemed to always be a struggle between including me and keeping me in my place. At times I felt controlled, excluded, and manipulated, and at other times, I felt respected and cared for.

I remember one particular meeting that the four of us planned for our sales leadership team of 200. While the agenda was evenly distributed, on the day of the event, my colleagues went over their allotted time and pushed us up against a hard stop. Because I was last, I was left in a position where my ability to perform and capitalize on the moment was jeopardized.

After walking off the stage, our Senior Vice President said, "We're going for a walk."

I'll never forget his words. "You are capable of rising above the fray in those situations. Never let anybody steal your peace." When things happen that you didn't plan for, stay the course. Make appropriate adjustments, but do it with grace.

*Katinka*

# Bringing Your Brand to Life

Understanding your brand and communicating it to others is important. But you also have to actualize it — that is, translate it into action, truly live it, and sustain it over time. Kari Groh of The Timken Company spends significant time coaching executives and future leaders on using brand to their advantage. Kari shares her advice on how to actualize your brand so that you have tangible signs of success.

## *Actualizing Your Brand*

Tips on how to bring your brand to life from Kari Groh, VP of Communications | The Timken Company

Develop a lexicon of the phrases and descriptors that reflect the unique you and your leadership style. If your brand narrative depicts you as a business builder, then include words like *construct, fabricate, assemble, formulate, foundation, concrete,* and *blueprint.* If you're a trailblazer, then *scout, navigate, lead, survey,* and *track* are likely within your language set.

Then, embrace your narrative. Initially, do so by incorporating key words and phrases into everyday activities. Drive them into your performance plan and reviews. Ensure that they are well represented in your LinkedIn profile, bio, and résumé. Use them when talking with your team and colleagues, and purposefully edit them into your business correspondence. It may feel awkward at first, for it's easy to get stuck in tired corporate-speak. But you'll soon become fluent in this new language, giving you energy and quickly distinguishing you from your peers.

How will you know whether you've been truly successful in actualizing your brand? The first sign comes when you begin living your brand and assessing opportunities in the context of it. Another milestone achievement is when your brand narrative becomes your filter to determine where, and whether, you want to commit your personal and professional resources. The best indicator of success, however, is when you hear the echoes; your own descriptors coming from colleagues and managers as they observe you and your performance and results. That's sweet success!

When you drift off course, it's not always obvious. But there are things to watch for, such as an increased sense of anxiety and stress, or finding that you are a different person at work than at home. Often, it's your inner voice that will let you know.

"I think women are amazing at compartmentalizing, so it's easy to put the parts of our jobs into buckets. While I feel it's a hugely beneficial skill, it sometimes works against us," says Ann Fandozzi, CEO of ABRA Auto. "In a previous role, I was succeeding, developing teams that I loved, and mentoring people. Because these were all good, I could compartmentalize, even though my gut was telling me that I didn't fit. I started to question, 'Is it me? Maybe if I try it differently?'" However, she has learned,

**"Instincts at this level are fantastic, listen to them. The only time I look into the rearview mirror is when I should have made the decision to leave sooner because I wasn't listening to my inner voice."**

Sometimes, you may find that being true to yourself is really not working well — that the pressure to conform doesn't let up. If you are truly comfortable with who you are but your company clearly isn't, the problem may be that the organization's culture is simply not a good fit. If so, it may be time to find another place.

Is your work environment or company culture stopping you from bringing your A-game? That was certainly the case early in my career, as I tried to reinvent myself to fit into the old boys' network. You can be successful in those situations, but inside you will feel that something is not right. **If you try to force-fit yourself into a situation, it will affect every aspect of your life.**

The effects of a poor fit will be clear to those around you. "At one point, I was working for another company, and I was really stressed out," says Joan Wainwright, President, Channel & Customer Experience for TE Connectivity.

"My mother said to me,

*'You're a beautiful person on the outside, but you have become an ugly person on the inside.'*

"That was a wake-up call for me. Finding the right place with a culture that matches who I am works for me. That's the way I keep my authenticity and my brand."

# Q How do you balance being authentic with fitting into your company's culture?

**Kristi Hedges:** Authenticity isn't binary, but exists on a continuum. We make choices about how authentic we want to be, in what ways, and in which settings. We feel our best, our most confident and powerful, when we can show up as ourselves, able to live into our core values. But that said, we can also try on new behaviors, stretch ourselves, and add to our repertoires of what's authentic. There are also style issues around authenticity that reflect respect and trust. One of the ways that we show our trustworthiness is we model the culture. We say, "That's important to you, so it's important to me, and I'm going to do it." Ultimately, being authentic is about making choices. It's asking ourselves if we're acting in line with our core values, what's worth growing into, and what's too far from who we want to be.

—Kristi Hedges, Leadership Coach, Author, Speaker | The Hedges Company, LLC

**Robb Webb:** I've worked in four different industries. At Hyatt, we had a dress code to wear suits. We secured a change to wear jeans in the headquarters, which was the equivalent of burning the White House. It was because we looked at the workforce situation. We said, "You know what, use your brains. Use your judgment. Be respectful of other people. If people come to our hotel because our colleagues dress like this, then dress like that. If you know that we're having the President of Israel visiting, dress appropriately. If you can't figure that out, there's probably some other stuff you're screwing up as well that we'd like to know about."

—Robb Webb, Chief Human Resources Officer | Tenet Healthcare Corporation

# Elsa Amouzgar

*My mom always told me, "You need to be independent and make your own money, even if it's just to buy your lipstick."*

My 76-year-old mom went skiing this year with my 81-year-old stepdad. She never sits down. She is one of the biggest influences in my life. Born in the 1940s, she worked as a secretary to an international professional association.

She used to organize their annual congress each year in a different country and traveled to India, Australia, and Japan at a time when international travel was just beginning and very few women did it. She opened up my eyes to what's happening in the world, and probably that's what I wanted to pursue as well. In her time, she would make her money, but could not legally open a bank account when she had her first job without the authorization of her husband. That was just one generation ago.

*Elsa is the VP – General Manager of ManpowerGroup*

## No Guilt

When you get into middle and senior management, you have an opportunity to set the conditions. I hate to hear someone say, "It's terrible. I have to attend meetings at 7 pm because my boss wants it." I think it's important to actually say how you can or want to work and drive it. My team and my boss know that between 7 pm and 9 pm, that is the time with my husband and children. I don't think you should ask; I think you should take it.

You don't hear men ask authorization to go golfing on Friday afternoons. There's absolutely no reason to feel guilty when saying how you want to work. In fact, there are often opportunities we shy away from that we can actually make work. We were recently invited by a client to an executive golf event, only I don't golf. I just went. I said, "I'm going to join dinner, I'm going to join lunch, no problem, but I'll be there." There's no reason to not be part of these things.

Reflecting back, that's something that I've done over the past 20 years. I've taken the liberty to go to conferences, to go and have lunch with who I thought was important to have lunch with, or go to cocktails without asking, really. I think it's about grabbing the opportunity and showing the value of how you work rather than complain about things not happening to you.

# Standing Out in a Crowded Field

**I wish I had started much earlier on building my brand.** I worked long hours, head down, delivering projects for my company, and working in my particular department, but I didn't spend a lot of time on myself or my network. Even though innovation was something I saw as important, it wasn't until after the program that I identified this as a brand differentiator for me. IT, SAP implementations — I could do all of those standard technologies, but I realized that a differentiator for me was to go big on innovation. I questioned myself on what I could build in my brand and my profile that demonstrates I have that as a core, as part of me.

So, I went after it. I actually moved out of a very comfortable corporate park to move into a different space. I opened a development lab in Georgia Tech's Technology Square in downtown Atlanta, a high-profile, high-energy incubation center of many companies feeding off of each others' energy and connections. I am now so very connected with the technology community in Atlanta, and in the US more broadly, that not a week goes by where recruiters aren't calling me for executive IT positions. All I knew at the time was that I had to get out of my comfort zone.

The company I am with, a large FMCG [fast-moving consumer goods] company, was headed into a merger, and I knew the center of activity would move from Atlanta to London. I needed to proactively go after my future.

I decided on how I wanted to evolve my brand and communicate it differently. I changed my LinkedIn profile first, describing my passion, expertise, and focus on innovation, rather than my career path. I was starting to get invitations to appear on panels, and companies were contacting me about my comments on panels and then visiting our innovation lab.

**I became known for exactly what I wanted my brand to represent. I am now the innovation person that I always thought I would be.**

I think if there's something in your brand that you do well, and it can make you more valuable to your organization, then re-word it.

## Think bigger.

Siobhan Smyth
VP, Information Technology, Coca-Cola European Partners

# Q Can you evolve your brand over time?

**Jeanne Quirk:** Your brand doesn't have to be what the stereotype is of your role. Take my personal brand, as I'm responsible for mergers and acquisitions for our company. That's typically aligned with high-profile, high-intensity, high-risk, high-stakes, and usually high dollars. It attracts a certain type of person that people expect to be very competitive, very well-educated, very confident, and often full of themselves. Many people in my profession are quite arrogant.

My own personal brand is to be different. I want to be just as strong from the execution perspective as everybody else, but without the ego. I found that really trying to stay true to that has actually become a competitive advantage for our company. We won a deal recently because we were viewed as down-to-earth. I think that you can stay true to your brand, even if it's not the way everybody else in your field projects themselves.

—Jeanne Quirk, SVP Mergers and Acquisitions | TE Connectivity

**Sarena Lin:** First and foremost, you have to find out what your brand is in the eyes of those around you. It's absolutely critical to understand how people perceive you. Most of us underestimate how others see us.

I had a long career as a management consultant before joining Cargill about five years ago. When I first got here, everybody looked at me and said, "She is a consultant." For those of you in the corporate world, you know that when you are being labeled as a consultant, that's actually not a good brand.

How am I going to change my brand in a way that people understand who I am? That was just a professional career I had; it has nothing to do with my authentic self. First, I started telling people, "Consulting is part of my background, but not who I am as a leader. This is the value I bring to this organization." Once I articulated it, then I had to demonstrate it.

—Sarena Lin, President, Cargill Feed & Nutrition | Cargill

# Evolving Your Brand

Brands need to evolve over time, because you grow and change. As we get smarter about who we are and see where our gifts can provide the most value, then we can evolve our brands to continue to amplify those assets we have built and honed over the years. Siobhan Smyth shares (on page 41) how she realized she needed to zero in on her differentiator in the IT leadership space. She found there were lots of IT executives that knew how to manage and deliver IT integrations and programs. But she loved the innovation space and decided to carve this out for her specialty.

Being authentic is not always easy, but the courage to stay true to yourself has big payoffs for you in leadership AND life.

## Advice to My Younger Self

It's okay to be you. Be yourself and, in fact, evolve yourself. Don't be afraid of change or being different. It's okay to assert your viewpoints because even though that viewpoint is different, it's valuable. I had to overcome thinking I had to always fit in. I thought that my generation was going to be the generation where women were going to take the rightful place in company leadership. In some ways we have, but I don't think we have come as far as I expected. In today's world, different perspectives will make innovation better, will make companies better, will make change better, and will be the difference in making a company survive in this complex world.

**Jane Leipold**
**Retired SVP Human Resources | TE Connectivity**

Those who know others are intelligent;
those who know themselves are truly wise.
Those who master others are strong;
those who master themselves have true power.

— Lao Tzu

# Power

*I had been "in transition" (read: unemployed) for 11 months, and I needed to do something soon to provide for my family. I had several job offers, but I knew they weren't the right fit. I started exploring roles out of left field, including the CMO of a large funeral services and cemetery provider. With each month that went by, I began spiraling into self-doubt.*

# Where was the lifeline?

I did what had always served me well ... assembled my close advisors to help me get perspective. These allies knew me well, knew my capabilities, and knew my thought process. They cared deeply for me and my success. One suggestion was to hire a professional résumé writer who interviewed me for three hours. When the résumé came over email, I opened it and gasped, "Who is this?" And then I realized it was me, and everything was accurate. Someone else was seeing me in a way that I could not see myself. Getting "outside of myself" unlocked the spiral and allowed me to power into action. I knew I wanted to join a company aligned with my core values, AND I wanted a leadership role that utilized my gifts. I craved growth, so growth had to be the focus for my search. I was re-energized to own the process.

## What is Power?

Power is about sticking to your core values — those non-negotiables that give you the confidence to act with conviction. Your power comes from being intentional about where you are going and how you are going to get there. It's that inner force that helps you manage through your self-limiting beliefs, deploy your gifts to the fullest, face fears, and bounce back from failures. Power fuels you to stretch yourself and take risks so that you can grow.

---

# The Only Person Telling Me No Was Me

One of the things that held me back early on was that I found myself in the business world, and I had no business background. How could I be a leader in a commercial enterprise without actually having any commercial experience? There was no one telling me that except myself. Everybody else was telling me that I could be a business leader. They were offering me opportunities in marketing and in sales.

The only person telling me no was me, and I usually find I'm doing that before I let somebody else tell me no. When I think that there is a wall, or something that can't be pressed, I just have to take a step back. Am I the one telling me no, or has someone else really told me no? I always like a challenge, so ironically, I'm far better at going after something to prove someone else wrong.

**If other people tell me no, I'm going to find a way.**

**It's when I tell myself no that I suddenly get really stuck.**

### Shanna Wendt
**VP of Communications | Coca-Cola European Partners**

# Power Suck

When confronted with a hard decision or a challenge, it's easy to curl up into your comfort zone. Unfortunately, your comfort zone includes your internal rationalizations why things didn't go your way — your self-limiting beliefs. When power suck happens to someone else, you recognize it quickly. You can coach them through that space where their Inner Critic takes over, helping them reframe those negative thoughts to gain confidence again. You feel good when you can get them over a hurdle.

## *That Bad Inner Critic*

It's much harder to recognize your own Inner Critic, that self-talk that holds you back. "I'm not ready for that position yet." "I don't have anything worth adding to the conversation." I used to be a superstar at negative self-talk, and while it never completely goes away, understanding your power base and how to use it to reframe your thoughts can minimize the Inner Critic's voice.

Our belief systems are formed at an early age. How you see yourself in the world, how you view your capabilities, even how you move through your company or navigate your leadership track are based on these beliefs. I grew up as a chubby child and am still self-conscious about my weight, even after conquering that issue. Years later, I was in my boss's office. We were disagreeing on something, and he commented that my arms crossed across my torso suggested I was not open to his idea. Without thinking, I said, "That's not true. I grew up as 'Carol the Barrel,' and I always hold myself this way to cover it up." At a very early age, you adopt a belief that being yourself is somehow not enough.

When you allow self-limiting beliefs to "rent space" in your head, it creates a conversation that can spiral you downward. Women are typically more likely to blame themselves for things that don't go well, where men will do the opposite — they may blame someone else, the situation, or even the entire environment.

# Kathryn Beiser

*Growing up, my two brothers dared me to take on many new challenges. Now if somebody says I can't do something, my first reaction is, 'Well, why not give it a try?'*

I think that being pleasant and professional is part of my nature. But I've realized I don't always have to be agreeable, and not everyone is going to like me. When I try to just please people, it becomes a very personal thing, as opposed to being focused on the job at hand. You have to really focus on the professional, which was a really tough thing to learn as a young woman who had been taught to not make waves and to be nice.

**From a business perspective, you will never achieve your goals if you're just trying to please people. You have to decide what's best and then run with it, bringing as many people along as possible.**

Earlier in my career, an incredible opportunity came my way and I thought, "Wow, bigger company, broader responsibilities." The job seemed a natural

*Kathryn is the Global Chair, Corporate Practice, of Edelman*

stepping stone in my career progression, and I loved the enthusiasm my new boss had for the organization and the role I would play in it. Reality proved rather different, however. Within a year or so of joining the company, I realized that my boss and I had very different visions for my role. While the scope of my responsibilities was thoroughly articulated in my new job description, my day-to-day existence was quite different; in many ways, the role was smaller than my prior position. Clearly, it wasn't the right fit for me.

But because I hate to give up, I tried to make it fit anyway. **I thought if I could just make this human being happy, then I'd get some air cover so I could actually do the rest of the job.** I had worked with CEOs and presidents who had opinions, but were also great learners; leaders who valued advice and sought my counsel. But this particular person and I just weren't connecting, and nothing I tried improved the situation. I started to lose my mojo. It started affecting all aspects of my life. After months of making little progress, I finally realized it was not going to work.

This experience has taught me that when opportunity knocks, you really need to do your due diligence during the interview process. I think I got so caught up in the promise of the role that I missed (or ignored) some signs that perhaps, it wasn't going to be the right fit for me. You need to make sure your rational side kicks in and that you really dissect the pros and cons.

## Be clear on what you want and the desired outcome.

The opposite of people-pleasing is asking for what you want. When I was working for one of the big public relations firms in my 30s, I was given an opportunity to run a small chunk of a global piece of business under a managing director. It was about $300,000 worth of billings, that I grew to $1 million in one year. I went to the head of my group and I said, "Listen, what I did here, I can do globally. You need to give me a chance because the current director hasn't achieved that." He said, "Thank you very much, no." I said, "All right." I had an alternative. "So

how about you give me one more region and six months to see if I can build and deliver on that? If I do, then will you consider it?" He replied, "Absolutely." I continued, **"And will I get the managing director title?" He hesitated, "Well, you're a little young for that." I persisted, "No, I'm not. If I deliver, I'm ready for that."**

While I grew the business, it took longer than I had hoped to get the title. When I did, however, I found that my colleagues were probably more supportive because they saw I had been doing the job for months before I got the official recognition. I also learned some important lessons about balancing patience with my perseverance.

An essential part of becoming a leader and developing your career is understanding that everything doesn't come to you at once. You have to enjoy the moment and where you are in your career. You can't focus too much on not knowing whether you can do something or not. Just jump in and try it — and learn. That approach has shifted my career in ways I couldn't have foreseen.

## If I'm not learning, there's a lot of online shopping going on.

People ask me, "What was your plan? Did you always know that you wanted to be a Chief Communications Officer?" I've been very honest in saying, absolutely not. What I did know early on was what drove me. I know that I'm a learner. I have to keep moving and have challenging work to do. When I took my first Chief Communications Officer role, I took the step because I realized that it was an important growth opportunity. I thought, "Why not try? The worst thing that can happen is that I hate it. I can always figure something else out."

*Kathryn*

# Who's to Blame?

*I was playing golf at one of our corporate meetings. It was team play, and each foursome was being videotaped on the first tee for their first drive. One of my teammates, a Brit named Michael, teed up his ball, took out his driver, positioned himself over the ball without a warmup, and swung as hard as he could. He completely missed the ball and, without hesitation, looked straight into the video camera and said, "Tough course." While that was quite funny to the others in the foursome, the track that was running through my head was, "Wow, I'm not very good at golf and I hope I don't do that."*

Attribution is that social psychology that points to the cause of events or behavior. Many studies show women will revert to more internal attributions when faced with failure and men will use external attributions. Michael used external attribution.

## Moving Past Power Suck

Awareness of the different ways you limit yourself is the first step toward "powering on." Taking the time to reframe the limit is what Sarah Barron, Global Head of Talent and Leadership at Arla Foods, says helped her to move past a paradox in her mind.

> **"I always felt that I could not measure up to my colleagues because I didn't have the 20 years of experience in the HR field. I finally realized that my differences could bring a valuable perspective to our conversations because my experience base was so different. I had lots of value to add."**

Breaking down your barriers helps build your confidence.

In *The Confidence Code*, authors Katty Kay and Claire Shipman sought to understand why women seemed to have less confidence than men. They pored through research and the latest thinking on neuroscience, and interviewed successful women with varied backgrounds and experiences. They were trying to understand if confidence was in the DNA or if it could be developed. They actually arrived at a very simple yet profound definition of confidence.[1]

## Confidence *(noun)*

1. The ability to turn thought into action.

I think this rings true with so many leaders. How often have you been in a meeting, thinking you wanted to say something, and didn't? Minutes later, someone else offers the exact idea, and you start kicking yourself for missing the boat. Getting it from your head to your mouth can be hard!

Confidence can be compromised when fear raises its head. The fear of failure can cause you to not take action or to dig for lots of data before making a decision, believing more information will increase your success rate. Fear stalls, and can even prevent your progress.

## Don't Agonize over Decisions

Ronee Hagen, retired President and CEO of Polymer Group, Inc., shares this advice:

"**Reasonably smart will get the job done. You're never going to have perfect information. You can get through a maze pretty quickly by not spending a lot of time agonizing over each decision. Momentum is important. With it, you have the time to adjust and move forward. That is working smart.**"

## Confidence. One Step at a Time.

To strengthen confidence, you need to put it to work in small doses, over long periods of time. You don't have to be super confident all of the time, but you do need to practice confidence. It means being intentional about taking one step at a time.

## Be Realistic to Be Resilient

Another way to work smart is to approach problems with the reality that not everything is going to be perfect nor needs your full attention.

"When I'm faced with a problem and the next steps aren't obvious, I think about the future. What will this situation look like six months, or a year, from now? Will this problem be as important in the future as it seems today? Sometimes a situation can be more difficult in the moment, but it's actually not something that's going to have real impact in the long run. Try to 'time test' situations to determine how much energy you should expend on them. **If it's not that important, then conserve your energy for things that really matter.** Having a bigger store of energy helps me to be more resilient and impactful when it counts."

**—Canda Carr**
**VP of Global Channel Sales | TE Connectivity**

# Anne Hill

## Always think big and go after it.

I do what I do because I always wanted to be financially independent and able to look after myself. It always seemed to me that, if I was going to spend my efforts in paid employment, I may as well try and maximize my earning potential.

**My father used to say, "The only difference between a rut and a grave is the depth." Don't get into a rut doing the same old stuff because you may as well lie in your grave.**

I do HR because I am curious about the psychology of why people behave the way they do and how organizations work. That goes way back to university days when I completed a Bachelor of Science and Economics where I had a mixture of economics, psychology, sociology, and all those fun things. The organizational dynamics were always the most interesting part to me.

I started work in the early 1980s in the United Kingdom. In those days, the glass ceiling was well and truly in place, but HR was an accepted pathway for women to establish themselves, right up to the most senior levels of the organization. To me, it was the pathway to success that combined my overall interest with my need to be financially independent. It has proven to be the case.

*Anne is the SVP and Chief Human Resources Officer at Avery Dennison.*

## High Tension = High Growth

I was recruited to my first top HR job for a biotechnology company. I had four children at the time; my twins were the youngest, at 5 years old. I commuted for two years between San Francisco and Los Angeles and was totally supported by a great husband.

I know there were things that I was good at, and also things that I was shockingly bad at, because I was ill prepared. It was a tough situation. The company got itself in trouble, and so the CEO and the board were not particularly happy with each other. It was a very tough first "top" role for me, but I learned a lot and would highly recommend gaining some experience with a company going through a major challenge as a way of honing your skills. You stand much better prepared for the ups and downs of the business cycle.

**I don't ever feel I have to prove why I'm in this job because, come the day that somebody doesn't think I should be, they'll fire me.**

Having roles with adversity are big learning moments. What I've learned is that unless somebody's suffered physically, these things are not the end of the world. Part of my brand is the ability to keep calm when things are going to hell, and to get everybody to see it through a broader context than just living in the moment. I have always admired and learned from leaders who lift you up when you've screwed up or, when times are tough, can show you the way.

Since the kids were born, I've always traveled 50% of my time globally, and I have to be very organized around that. I've always had the belief, maybe somewhat naively, that I could have my cake and eat it, too. But to do it, you have to have clear boundaries, a first-class team around you, and a support structure in place for the family.

When I joined Avery, I felt so much better prepared for the top role.

The transition required me to learn a new industry and, most importantly, how the company made money. Understanding the important indicators, such as the manufacturing or our customer base, is different than the R&D of a biotech company. My priority agenda is always linked back to the business agenda and what the CEO needs to accomplish.

## The Need for Empathy

Being in the HR function, we spend a lot of time interviewing candidates and assessing if they fit. Making sure their experience, through the hiring process, is a good one is so important. I say to my HR team, "You should be fired and have to go and look for a job, and then you'll know what it's like for all these candidates that come in and see us from the other side of the table."

# Power On

### The Intentional Mindset

In 2012, McKinsey & Company published a study called, "Unlocking the Full Potential of Women at Work." The study points to four barriers that impede women from advancing through the corporate pipeline: structural obstacles, lifestyle choices, institutional mindsets, and individual mindsets.[2] The fourth barrier is the most intriguing to me. I find it astounding that more than half of the successful women interviewed for the study felt they had held themselves back from accelerated career growth with self-imposed barriers.

This reminds me of an interview I facilitated with pro golfer and winning Ryder Cup captain Paul Azinger. When he agreed to lead the underdog U.S. Ryder Cup squad in 2008, Paul described how he immediately set out to "control the controllables." He couldn't control the course or the weather, but he had many things he could control. He honed in on the individual mindset of each golfer to determine his pairings and emphasized team support. Paul's meticulous attention to detail freed his golfers of distractions and put them at ease. With the controllables controlled, the 2008 U.S. Ryder Cup team triumphantly ended a decade of European dominance.[3]

Of the four factors listed in the McKinsey & Company study, individual mindset stands out as the one controllable.

**We have the power to be intentional, communicating what we want, what we need, and even what we aspire to.**

Kathryn Beiser, Global Chair for the Corporate Practice at Edelman, describes how she set her intentions with her boss early in her career for a stretch role. She then proceeded to be very clear about asking for the title and the pay that went with it, if she delivered (see Kathryn's story beginning on page 48).

### Act Like It!

I have experienced, firsthand, how setting intentions can create possibilities. When you **adopt the mindset of already having the next job,** it removes barriers and can be an outright game-changer.

Not long ago, I received a phone call from an executive, just after she had concluded a meeting with the CEO. She relayed her conversation with me. "He said he was restructuring his executive team and was considering me for the Chief Strategy Officer role. I didn't know he thought of me with that potential." My reply to her was this. "The good news is, he has tipped his hand by sharing his thoughts. Now the course of action is to **act like you already have the job, because it is now yours to lose.** From this point forward, take every opportunity to provide your ideas on strategy. At every meeting, insert yourself into conversations that allow you to share your vision of the strategy. They will be clear how intentional your desires are for this position, and your actions will align with your words. The CEO can now only take it away from you." A few months later, she called to say she had the role.

This approach has worked for a significant number of our Signature graduates. You may not want the CEO role, but you can adopt this mindset for the role that you want to have, or in ways that expand the role you currently have. **You are now intentionally positioning yourself for more growth in an area where you have your greatest passion.**

# REFRAME
# "I'm Not Ready" to "I'm Smart Enough"

### THE YOUNG PROFESSIONAL

I'm not ready.

I only have **80**% of the capabilities I think I need for that next role.

## VS.

### THE EXPERIENCED PROFESSIONAL

I'm **50**% prepared for the role, but realize I'm smart enough to use my team to learn what I need to succeed!

*SOURCE: Survey of 60 Executives from The Signature Program*

# Joan Wainwright

*You practice, you do well. You practice more, you do even better. You practice a lot, you win!*

My father was a dairy farmer and my mom was a secretary for the president of a company. Very different worlds, but they both instilled confidence in me that I could be anything and do anything I wanted. They also taught me the value of hard work. My mother would go to work, even if there was a blizzard. She had an incredible work ethic. My father did, too, as you can imagine. He milked our cows twice a day, seven days a week. I had the responsibility for taking care of seven horses. That taught me a sense of responsibility. I didn't have a back-up who would come in and feed them, clean the stalls, get water for them, brush them, or ride them. It was me. I showed the horses, and that helped me understand that practice led to winning, which I really liked.

I joined TE Connectivity as Senior Vice President of Communications. We're a very blue-collar, roll-up-your-sleeves, low-ego company. That's a culture that fits for me. I worked for a company before that wasn't a fit for me. I didn't like the people. I didn't like the attitude. **It was an organization where people would get in a room, nod politely at each other and say, "Yeah, I agree," and then they'd go out in the hallway and say, "I'm not doing that."**

*Joan is the President, Channel and Customer Experience, at TE Connectivity*

**Finding the right place with a culture that matches who I am works for me; that's the way I keep my authenticity and keep my brand.**

Early in my tenure at TE, our CEO invited me to have lunch with him. I prepped a lot for our meeting. I had lists, a notebook, and even a PowerPoint deck. **He looked at me and asked, "What are you doing?" He said, "I only wanted to have lunch."** I think once you get to the point where you realize you don't have to have all the answers, it's incredibly liberating. I think you can bring more of yourself to conversations versus "Oh, my gosh, I haven't studied up on that particular topic."

When you get to that point, it is so much fun versus trying to be all buttoned up and having all the answers. Trying to be perfect is tiring. It takes a lot of energy. I am in a job now where I surely didn't have all the answers when I started.

One day, our CEO came back from visiting a number of our distributors and during a staff meeting said, "It's clear we're not leveraging our size and scale with our distributors. I want someone to run a task force and take a look at this."

Of course, we're all looking at our shoes. **I remember looking out the window, thinking, "Please, don't pick me. Please, don't pick me."** He turned to me and said, "Joan, I want you to lead this."

It turned out to be a great experience because I just listened to people. What I heard was consistent between our distributors and our internal people. And I realized we needed a distribution strategy and a business unit to run this. Because of the work I had done on the task force, our CEO saw I was passionate about the business, I cared about it, and I was able to take a fresh look at something that needed a fresh look. He offered me the opportunity to run the business.

Of course, I was scared. I didn't know exactly what I was doing, but I felt comfortable that our CEO had confidence in me and had my back. I felt like he threw me into the deep end of the pool, but was standing on the side with a life preserver, in case I needed it. To be successful, I needed to draw on my network of people who had my back. These were people I could go to and say, **"You know what, I need help on this particular project or this particular day."** You've got to have your network of people that you trust and whom you can ask for help.

You need to surround yourself with friends and past or current colleagues to help you navigate unknown territory. When I was new on the TE Leadership Team, the only other female on the team had been there a while. She was the person I could talk to.

**She would watch me walk toward a landmine and tap me on the shoulder and tell me to "come on back, you are about to step into something."**

*Joan*

---

## Realistic Leadership

You can be positive, but you also need to be receptive to hearing, and admitting, that things aren't necessarily great. That is not being negative. It is being realistic, which means recognizing a problem and looking for a solution — not wallowing in the negative. I love people who solve problems; someone who comes in and says, "This is the bad news, but here are five solutions or three options." That's leadership.

## Creating Capacity

Moving into bigger roles, traveling the globe, managing more people, and creating time for family and friends requires a lot of capacity. These big jobs demand physical and emotional energy.

**There are certain people that seem to have amazing capacity to take things on, while others get crushed by it.**

The Signature faculty has spent time delving into this challenge. Given that you have the competencies, abilities, and accountabilities for these types of roles, how do you find more capacity? In some ways, you can think about yourself like a factory. If you need more manufacturing capacity, you try to eliminate waste so your factory can be more streamlined and efficient in the same number of hours. I find that everyone inadvertently builds a lot of waste into their lives. Calendars are filled with wasted hours given to projects that don't matter or that don't really need YOU on them. Schedules contain travel when travel is not really (truly) necessary, or time with people who don't impact what you are working on.

## A Different Kind of Work

Finding capacity doesn't mean adding more hours to the job. As you move up the leadership path, you need to remember that at each level you are being paid for different capabilities. I often hear women leaders admit to holding on to some of their previous responsibilities when they move to a new role. As a result, they end up holding too many spinning plates. It doesn't take long for one of those plates to fall.

Early in my career, my sisters and I went to visit our older brother in his new high-rise in downtown Cleveland. He is the oldest of seven siblings, and the only brother, and we were quite excited to see him in

## What the Hours You Work Say About You

You cannot limit a company's growth based on the number of hours you're going to work. I understand being available 24/7; that's the nature of the job. When you're doing a deal, for instance, you may work 24 or 48 hours in succession. But if you are consistently working lots of hours or coming in on Saturdays, you are in over your head. And the signals you give as a leader are very important.

This isn't about being altruistic. Unless you can design jobs that are reasonable for people to accomplish, you have failed the organization. Your organization cannot succeed if you burn people out and have them showing up just to do meaningless work.

**Ronee Hagen**
Retired President & CEO | Polymer Group, Inc.

action. We arrived on the top floor to discover there were only a few offices, each with lots of square footage. When we got to his office, we saw only a few things on his desk. My 17-year-old sister asked, "Yank, why is your desk so clean?" I will never forget his reply.

**"By the time things reach me, the work has been done."**

*That comment hit home.*

# At the executive levels, it's NOT about doing MORE work. It's about doing DIFFERENT work.

You are now being paid for your judgment and your expertise at decision-making. You are being paid to develop, mentor, and sponsor rising leaders. As a leader, if you do not have the time to think, strategize, make decisions, or extend your presence into the community, then you have probably not figured out how to delegate and involve others in the work that is now theirs to do. We learned in Chapter One this was the very thing that kept Matt Schuyler, CHRO of Hilton Worldwide, from being promoted (see page 14). He did not think about "The Brand of You."

## *Managing You, Inc.*

Creating more capacity involves prioritizing and managing the things that impact you, including your health, your sleep, and even all of the relationships you keep. One of the ways to increase capacity is to make sure you have the right team at work and the right support structure in your personal life. Having trusted people around you is critical.

Ann Fandozzi, CEO of ABRA Auto, has spent years developing talent that she calls the 0.0001%. She says she could not be a CEO unless she had this kind of team around her.

**"The ability to surround myself with incredible people increases my confidence and increases my ability to be successful."**

Developing high-performing teams is not easy, but it is certainly rewarding for all involved. And it increases the capacity of everyone, not just you!

> **"If you align your team based on their strengths and have a high sense of trust, then the sky's the limit, due to the strength and capacity of your team. It's easier for everyone to achieve more when they work together. When you have high-performing teams, you never forget the experience."**
>
> **Patty Babler**
> VP, NA Regional HR Solutions Lead | Cargill

# Leslie Pchola

## Get in the habit of stretching yourself and moving faster through different experiences.

When an opening came up that I was qualified for early in my career, I didn't get the position. I finally had the courage to ask somebody why they hadn't thought of me. For the last 30 years of my life, I've remembered their response.

### "You never expressed an interest. You've got to take the initiative to go after something, if you want it."

We're so afraid to take risks. Sometimes you've just got to stick your neck out. You just have to be sure it's not too far.

When a professor approached me looking for an analyst to work in the hospitality division of an accounting firm, I was flattered to be asked. I didn't want to *not* be considered because of what I didn't know, so I said, "Of course I'm used to doing spreadsheets and analyses, and I would do an excellent job." Three days into my new job, what do I get asked to do? Right. So that night, I call a couple of friends and ask if they could help me out. That was the first time I really had to recognize that asking for help, as embarrassing as it seemed at the time, was really the smartest thing to do. I buckled down and, with their guidance, taught myself how to use the tools I *supposedly* already knew. Taking risks will not always turn out this positively (I did keep that job). Sometimes you will fail. But when you win, it's a great confidence builder.

The more you adapt to change and the more you pick up the pace, the easier it gets.

Things that expose me to other areas of my company energize me. I love work groups and projects that have nothing to do with my field and that get me thinking outside the box. I thrive on the change that happens.

I was brought up with the idea that, if you work hard and keep your head down, people will notice you because of your results. I was always the first one in, last one out.

*Leslie is the Area VP, Operations S.E. of Hilton Worldwide*

# How do you create more capacity?

**Linda Knoll:** I'm not really sure that you necessarily create capacity because, for the most part, it is already there. You just have to learn to tap into it and recognize that none of us accomplish anything on our own. You've got to lead more and directly manage less. That's the way you really handle more responsibility. You've got to entrust others to manage the day to day. You've got to find a sense of being able to really smell what's relevant, what you personally need to get involved with. Leave the rest in the capable hands of your team.

—Linda Knoll, Chief Human Resources Officer | CNH Industrial, N.V. and Chief Human Resources Officer | Fiat Chrysler Automobiles, N.V.

**Abbe Luersman:** No leader really has everything. The best surround themselves with other people who fill their gaps. The key is to recognize your incompleteness and establish a complete team. Leveraging the strengths and energy of each individual on the team makes a difference. Not everyone has to be *the* very best at what they do, but they all have to be committed to what they're doing. Leveraging the strength and energy of the team as a whole is what creates excess capacity to deliver.

—Abbe Luersman, Chief Human Resources Officer | Ahold Delhaize

**Devry Boughner Vorwerk:** There are three key components needed to create capacity. It comes down to partnership, delegation, and prioritization.

Whether it's at home or in the workplace, you need partnerships. And they take work. There is no such thing as balance, so you need a partner where you both give and take by taking a holistic approach to your life.

In the workplace to gain capacity, you have to delegate, which can be the best way to achieve. I can do all of those things, but I don't have to. I need workplace partnerships to be successful.

Then it gets to prioritization, which means having a certain amount of forgiveness that I'm not going to be able to do it all. I really have to be focused on a key set of priorities in the workplace and in the home space.

—Devry Boughner Vorwerk, Corporate VP, Global Corporate Affairs | Cargill

# Leticia Goncalves

*Sometimes, we are the limitations in our lives and our careers because we try to make decisions based on old paradigms, or where we've been, instead of trying to project a new future.*

I had been working for Monsanto for 10 years in Brazil, and when I started looking at my career, my goal was to be a first-line manager or supervisor. I never thought I had potential to go beyond that, or maybe I didn't have the ambition or willingness to take it further. I came from a very simple, middle-class family.

The country lead at that time came to me and said, "We'd like to consider you for a role in St. Louis because we see potential in you, we want to further develop you, and we want you to have a headquarters experience."

*Leticia is the President, Europe and Middle East at Monsanto*

My first reaction was no. **I cannot entertain moving away from Sao Paulo and my family, and my husband has his own business. I'll never move away from Brazil.**

He told me not to say no yet, and go home and talk to my husband and consider a "what-if" scenario, on what that would look like, if I were to accept. I look back at that conversation and realize he was a good leader.

After a few days of difficult conversations, we went from "no way" to "maybe," and then to "at least let's explore a little bit more." I ended up being offered the position and accepting the opportunity, and that decision changed the course of my career, and our mindset of how we were going to raise our family.

We discovered a new world in the US and our two children were born there. My career started flying — I was learning how decisions were made in the headquarters, developing a stronger network, and enjoying the life experiences, as well. Things started happening for me.

**You cannot be effective in your career if you don't have your life in the right order and your support system intact.**

Years later, when I was offered the role to lead Europe, it became easier to entertain the possibility because the first experience of discovery had been so positive. I learned not to use my own bias to make a decision, but be willing to listen to other people that I trust.

But through that journey, if it was not for having good cultures, good mentors, and external advisors to boost my own confidence and create that "you-can" mentality, I probably would not have accepted many different roles in my career. I had to have a lot of people giving me the confidence I didn't have on my own. As I progressed and learned that my leadership can make a difference in people's lives, I built my confidence.

## Demonstrate Your Value

As I gained the confidence and desire to advance in my career, I began making my interest known for bigger roles. First, I would use examples of how I would approach that next role. I began acting as if I had the role during our leadership team conversations, so they could see I had a bigger perspective. Second, I clearly showed I had interest, not by being impatient or lacking commitment to my current role, but by saying, "I would like to progress in my career, and here are some of the things I like doing, and these types of roles would allow me to do this."

I am careful not to suggest that I am entitled to the role, but to convey what I could bring to the role and how that might benefit the company. For me, there needs to be a win-win in the conversation.

## The Growth Pain of Leadership

When you start to have too much confidence in yourself, you start using your own models that work. You miss opportunities to grow and use others' insights to reinvent yourself and become a more complete leader.

I learned that you grow the most in vulnerable times or in times where you're stretched. **If you're feeling too comfortable, it's because you're not challenging yourself enough, either because the role is not too big or you're not approaching the role as big as you could.** You need to be feeling a little bit of pain. I like feeling a lot of pain, because then I feel I'm growing. This is the growth pain of leadership.

It's not negative; it's constructive. It will take you to a better place. When you are in this moment, you need to create a plan to get you through the journey. Often, the biggest growth pain comes in the first 90 days of a new job. You should build a holistic plan with key milestones that consider not only what you want to accomplish, but how you want to be feeling through the journey. Surround yourself with strong, trust-filled relationships that provide fresh perspective. You need these other eyes to keep you on track to use the growth pain to the right outcome.

**It's easy to be a good leader in good times, but when things get rough, leadership is at a premium.** I have to stay true to my core values, my family, and my faith.

*Leticia*

# Marilyn Skony Stamm

## *Being successful in a role is all about having the confidence to improve your weaknesses and the work ethic to do it.*

extremely important, but so is the willingness to do what's necessary to make sure you fill the role.

When I started my career, I had a Master's, but not an MBA. I recognized that there were certain areas that I needed to supplement, like accounting and marketing, so I went to night school. At Kellogg, I took the courses that I felt were necessary to achieve the goals I had set for myself. Being successful in any role is all about having the confidence to improve your weaknesses and the work ethic to do it.

I've always taken non-traditional roles for women. My first position was as a foreign exchange trader. Back then, there were only two of us in the United States. Now I'm CEO of an international manufacturing business which produces industrial and commercial heating, ventilation, and air conditioning equipment, chimneys, and flues, and 98% of the people are male. I'm usually the only female in the room, but I never let my gender limit me.

You can learn more about a job, a division, or a position from the people doing it than you can from sitting upstairs talking to your peers. My first management position was in a foreign exchange trading operation. By spending time with people in the back office, I showed them that I recognized their work and valued them. Leadership requires making sure that all the people involved in your business know they're important and feel supported, regardless of where they stand on the corporate ladder.

I grew up with two extremely hardworking parents. My dad was a World War II veteran. My mom was born in Munich, Germany, and came to this country as his war bride. My parents built an environment around the belief that if you work hard, put your nose to the grindstone, and get yourself an education, there is no limit to what can be achieved in this country, the land of opportunity. It wasn't enough to just do a job; you had to do the best you could.

Whenever potential promotions came up, I stepped forward. I may not have always felt fully prepared for the role, but I always felt a great sense of confidence that if I had to learn something new, I could do it. Confidence is

*Marilyn is the CEO & Director of Stamm International Corp.*

# Q How do you build high-performing teams?

**Siobhan Smyth:** Sometimes you'll inherit a team, and you get a diverse mix. Earlier in my career, I jumped too quickly to get rid of people because I didn't feel that they fit in, or they weren't aligning with my idea of the organization. I learned that a lot of times, it's more about just finding where people are strong and using those strengths to best leverage them within your team. Bringing out the best in somebody is how you create a perfect fit for your team that you would never be able to find through hiring.

I found diversity is critical, especially for people that work for me that are directors over large areas. They tend to hire people that are just like them. I'm not talking about gender or ethnicity. They'll have the same exact personality. The introverts hire the introverts. The accountant-type people hire the accountant people. The gregarious, outgoing people hire the gregarious, outgoing people. What you find is, as they start to collect in large groups, it's not good. I make everybody cross into different interview groups and make sure that they have a diverse type of person on the team, as well. It's something that's very difficult, but makes for a better team performance.

—Siobhan Smyth, VP Information Technology | Coca-Cola European Partners

**Susan Huppertz:** It's more difficult to lead a diverse group. You have to work a lot harder to ensure engagement and coordination. I'm a person who loves quantification. I want to get it down to the numbers. I want to be able to measure it, and there's an element of a team dynamic that you just can't measure. It's a feeling you have of how things are working. I think that's where you need to take a step back and say, "How well are we working together? Is everyone engaged? What are we achieving?" You have to actively manage that team. So it's a feeling that you have, then it's your intervention to ensure that every person on your team is in the right context to deliver and support others.

—Susan Huppertz, VP Global Operations | TE Connectivity

**Sonya Roberts:** Creating high-performing teams is more than just getting the right people in place. You have to work on being a team. The expectations of what high performance looks like need to be understood. In our division, we turned the book by Patrick Lencioni, *The Five Dysfunctions of a Team*,[4] into "The Five Functions of a Great Team." We worked through scenarios of each function, talked about behaviors we would need to demonstrate, and found ways to measure our team effectiveness. I've never been on a team where we were so deliberate about working on teaming. For example, we reached a level of trust where we provided feedback to each other … in the team meetings. Wow! It was a great learning experience that I highly recommend for others, if you're on the right team.

—Sonya Roberts, President of Cargill Growth Ventures & Strategic Pricing, Cargill Protein | Cargill

## Give Them Space

Does this scenario sound familiar? Your direct report comes into your office and shares an idea that is 80% baked. Instead of asking questions, or just providing encouragement, the tendency is to jump in and tell them how they get it to 100%. Once you have done that, you have taken ownership of the solution, and your employee has likely lost the enthusiasm to do anything more with the idea. Giving too many details or advice on what to do can demotivate your team.

So take the positive approach, like Linda Knoll, CHRO of CNH Industrial, N.V. and CHRO of Fiat Chrysler Automobiles, N.V. Read her philosophy on giving people space in her story starting on page 116.

# "If you give your people SPACE, they will FILL it."

---

# What Is a Career Story?

## Don't close doors on yourself. Other people will close them soon enough.

I used to work for somebody for whom I loved working. He told me, "You might have three or four career stories in your lifetime, if you're lucky." I asked, "What's a career story?" He said, "You've heard them. Most of the people you enjoy interviewing tell them. They don't just give you goofy answers, they're saying, 'Let me tell you about this time this really interesting thing happened and then I ... .' That's a career story. Career stories don't come looking for you. You have to take the opportunity to live one when you see it."

### Robb Webb
#### Chief Human Resources Officer | Tenet Healthcare Corporation

# Know Your Shelf Life

It's tough to stay in your Power Zone when you sense that the job, the company, or the tenure in your role is just not right. You get a nagging feeling that you are "off," but can't put your finger on why.

As I was listening to my co-facilitator during a training session, I heard her say to the group, "You have to know your shelf life." That phrase smacked me to full awareness. While I had not been at this company for too long, the merger with another company changed the culture. My diminished comfort level with the new culture also diminished my power. Signs for reaching shelf life may appear for a while, but we often try to convince ourselves we have ways to "fix" the situation.

Since that time, I have queried many executives about the signs they've identified for when they were losing power. Here are some of the answers to:

## How do you know when you have reached your shelf life?

*"My learning curve had gotten flat. I was no longer growing and learning, and I was feeling a bit too comfortable in what I was doing every day. I need tension on my curve. I get much more energy from the steep part of that learning curve."*

*"I was losing energy for the people I worked with. My attention span for others was waning, and my impatience for things to get done had actually decreased. I was in status quo ... and it was not bothering me."*

*"The company values and dreams were no longer the same as mine. My alignment with where the company was going and their aspirations for the business no longer meshed. It's hard to play a leadership role when those are not aligned."*

*"I had the 'Sunday night' syndrome — that feeling that my Monday morning was more routine, and that I was missing that 'can't wait to get to the office and get started' kind of feeling. I couldn't find the mojo."*

When shelf-life signs start to appear, you should listen to them. You will have your best leadership moments when you can bring your passion and your energy with you. When you show up with your A-game every day, you inspire others around you to do the same.

## You need
### to have energy, to give energy.

# Marcia Avedon

*You have times when you have to choose — are you going to be on the sidelines or are you going to let your voice be heard?*

When you get to the most senior levels, people hold you to a different standard. Suddenly, you are a role model, not only on getting results, but on how results should be achieved.

I began my career as an industrial organizational psychologist, a specialist and an expert in leadership and organization development. The team I led were all of that same ilk. My first stretch leadership assignment was to run an HR organization for a large strategic business unit. The role encompassed a lot of things I had never dealt with before, like unions and global operations, and serving on a cross-functional business team. After a couple of cycles in that job, I realized that not only was I a leader, but that I actually *enjoyed* leadership.

**It was kind of an "aha" that I'm a business leader first and I happen to have some expertise in certain sub-disciplines.**

That was a big turning point for me. I loved being able to take a strategic perspective and connect different aspects of the organization with different

*Marcia is the SVP, Human Resources, Communications & Corporate Affairs at Ingersoll Rand*

opportunities, to lead change, and to bring about positive outcomes for the organization and the people. Even today, I'm still both studying leadership and practicing it. Being on the board of the Center for Creative Leadership, I get to hear about all the latest research in cross-cultural leadership and leadership development. While this knowledge is interesting, it is wisdom accumulated through experience that helps when it comes to the tough choices.

For me, tough choices are when there are either two good, or two poor, options. Either you have to have some way to decide between good competing alternatives, or you have to pick the "lesser of two evils." The key is to know what matters most, both to you and the other stakeholders in the situation. I often find I go back to, what's the core principle, or what would potentially set a precedent that later I'd look back on and not feel good about. In my decision-making, I remain true to my principles, while upholding my company's code of conduct and ethics.

Sometimes, the real purpose and what really matters are not always clear. Sometimes as leaders, we get confused or distracted. In these cases, I seek advice and counsel from others, including from individuals I think may have an opposing view. I say, "Here's what I'm thinking. I have a feeling you might not agree with me, so I really want to understand why that is."

## I'm not fearful about being the dissenter in a conversation. I'll speak my mind, even if I don't think others will necessarily see my point of view right away.

That dialogue reinforces for me why my choice is the right one, or at least, if I'm not going to waver, it lets me know where I'm going to have to deal with opposition or handle change management issues. Sometimes I find that dialogue even helps me build a coalition.

Recently, some legislation passed in the dark of the night affecting the lesbian, gay, bisexual, and transgender (LGBT) community. Someone in Washington sent a note to my CEO, who was on vacation out of the country, looking

for us to oppose the passing of the legislation. I got a message from my boss asking me what's going on. My gut had already told me this was something, we as a company, needed to take a stand on, rather than be silent. In his absence, people were looking to me, as the head of HR and Communications, to make a decision on behalf of the company. We only had a short window of time in which to respond.

## If you don't have ultimate authority for the whole company, and it's a decision you're making on the company's behalf, then create a coalition.

I wanted to be true to my values and principles, and I wanted to check in to make sure I would have a coalition of support if I did what I thought was best. I started talking to other executives, straight men primarily, to listen to their perspectives on whether taking a stand was the right thing to do from a principles standpoint, and whether it was good for our company and the economy. The consensus was that, in our opinion, it was a discriminatory piece of legislation. I checked in with a couple of lawyers to find out if I would be putting us out on a limb if I spoke up, or whether there would be a broader coalition of support.

We ended up signing a letter and speaking out with our stand on social media. This was something that mattered enough, even though it was a fairly politicized topic, to be brave and courageous and vocal. I was the one to put the company's name out there. And, fortunately, when the CEO came back a day later, I found out he was 100% behind my choice.

# Power Up

The ability to power up means taking that intentional mindset and actively owning your journey forward, knowing it will never be a smooth ride. Trying new things, reinventing your brand, actively listening to different perspectives helps you power up. It involves taking risks and stretching. But without any of this, you won't grow. Wisdom is earned through this process.

When you reach your shelf life, it doesn't necessarily mean it is time to leave your company. You can power up by creating new and expanded roles within your current company. Even lateral moves can pave the way for career advancement. The experiences, skills, and perspectives gained by taking on a lateral move can ultimately change your career trajectory. In today's business world, where organizations are flatter and climbing the ladder takes longer, many of our Signature alumni have found great value in gathering a variety of experiences through very different roles. One of our faculty CEOs said, **"Experientially, if it can move you into a new swim lane where you're learning more, that's hugely valuable."**

The term "lateral move" typically carries negative baggage, and yet most of the Wisdom Warriors in this book have chosen this very path at some point in their careers.

Kristie Dolan's story (on page 72) is packed with thoughtful planning and wisdom on how she has intentionally managed her career and personal development with a lateral move.

## Zigzag to Growth

I love the refreshing perspective shared by Kathryn Beiser, Global Chair of the Corporate Practice at Edelman, regarding her career path. She said, some of the best advice she had ever gotten was from her grandmother, who ran her own successful business.

**"Take a detour now and then to learn something new. If you keep going straight, eventually you're going to run right off the cliff."**

Kathryn took that wisdom to heart throughout her career. "If I was on a linear path, I might not have seen some of the opportunities that came my way. This zigzag approach really helped dimensionalize my experience, my skills, and, frankly, my perspective about my career."

## The Next, Next Job

Early in my career a gentleman said to me, "You should pick your next job not based on that job but based on the skills it's going to give you to help you in the job after that." That's made me be very purposeful. Choosing what's next is all about the next, next job. That works well for me because I've always had an incredibly long-term planning horizon. What's harder for me than figuring out my end game is figuring out the path to get there.

### Yvette Hill Smith
#### General Manager, Global Customer Support Services – C&E | Microsoft

## Making the Best Choice for You and Your Company

Not all lateral moves are alike. From our Signature discussions, I distilled some great questions to ask yourself when weighing the pros and cons of a move.

**How much trust do you have that the person/organization has your best interests at heart?** One executive relayed that he went kicking and screaming into two of the roles that turned out to be the best roles he ever had. But he trusted the leadership in his organization, knowing they were working on his behalf.

**Does the role offer an opportunity to enhance your skills and broaden your perspective, or is it just another role with a new cloak over it?** Be prepared to ask the questions to uncover the real opportunities, and use your network of colleagues and outside advisors to gain perspective on what that role might involve, and potentially deliver, to your skill set.

**How will your organization measure mastery, and what will be the expected time frame to achieve that goal?** Communicate your reason for taking the role with the people who have sponsored your move to this role, and get their agreement that the skills you will learn are the ones you will need to achieve the "next" role.

**How will this role expand your internal network of stakeholders and advocates?** It is easy to get "siloed" in an organization, especially if you have been there a long time. Making a move to another geography or business unit expands the breadth of relationships and can catalyze a career.

Lateral moves can also bring **exciting personal and family growth.** There's so much emphasis on the professional part of taking a new role that it can be easy to forget how this change will affect your personal life, especially those closest to you.

Kathleen Valentine, General Manager of Prescription Drug Monitoring and Toxicology at Quest Diagnostics, shared a story with The Signature Network that she was asked to move her family from New Jersey to California to oversee a tricky integration of an acquired company. It took a lot of encouragement from leadership for Kathleen to move her family, but she ultimately agreed. However, there was one condition: it would be for two years only.

When the two-year mark arrived, it was exactly as she wished. Her company knocked on her door and said, **"Kathleen, it's been two years. You can come back now."** But her family was thriving, they were loving the situation, and she had more work to do. She said, "No, thanks." After all was said and done, they stayed five years.

Lateral moves can rejuvenate and reignite your career excitement, and may even lead to a role you had not envisioned.

# Kristie Dolan

## It's more important to be interested than interesting.

Early in my career, I was assigned my first mentor, who was two levels above me. I was honored to go to lunch with him every few months. I learned a lot about him, and he was interesting, but what I realized over time is that he liked to talk. I knew a lot about him personally, but he completely lacked interest in me. Having been through that, I recognized that people sitting across the table want you to be interested in them. This has resonated with me throughout my career. It's natural for me that, when other people talk, the first thing that comes to my mind is something in my own experience worth sharing. But I just shut it off. I've had to develop the discipline of active listening.

## Mentor Vs. Coach

I used to think I was a great coach, and then I realized I wasn't. It was a breakthrough for me to understand and practice the difference. People would come to me with a problem, and I thought my role was to give suggestions, give the solution. I was typically more senior than that person, and I was in a role that they wanted to eventually get to. I was more of what I would call a "mentor."

The distinction is the coach doesn't actually need to know anything about what you do; they just simply need to be committed to your success. That's it. **Because as a coach, you're not giving them the answers, you're giving them the questions.** "Help me understand why you thought that, and then, what did you do next?"

The ultimate way to build trust is for that person on the other side of the relationship to believe you have their interests at heart. There's an element of getting to know people, as a whole person. There's a lot of active listening, understanding what drives them, understanding what they're measured on, understanding all those things so that you can frame your ask, or your discussion, around *their* perspective.

## How Do You Build Trust?

I think you have to see the person as a whole person. You have to understand how they come in every day and what they come in with. Then you have to go back to yourself, and say, "Am I truly vested in this person and their outcome? Am I genuinely coming from a place of caring and demonstrating that?" Anything short of that is inauthentic.

*Kristie is the General Manager- Women's Health of Quest Diagnostics*

# Owning Your Career

I was always on the commercial side of the business, and my boss's boss asked me to go into the back end of the business and join the procurement team. I just didn't see myself as a sourcing leader, and it wasn't where I wanted to go. He said, "Look, you're viewed as having a lot of energy, a lot of enthusiasm, and you're clearly moving things in a marketing perspective, but you haven't owned a number. You have to drive accountability. You have to drive hard negotiations. If you want to change the perception to someone who can grow beyond marketing, you need to take a different role." This was a lateral move, but I trusted his assessment.

Three things I learned through the process:

1. Get agreement on the purpose for taking the role. You need to understand what you are going in the role for, determine your critical success factors, and determine how you are going to exit;
2. Get specificity on the development goal. Clearly understand the expectation of the skills you need to learn to be able to "check this box" for your development; and
3. Make sure you have regular communications with the original sponsors who suggested you take this role. Relay what you are learning and what you are delivering for the company.

I entered the procurement role and did a very good job. After 18 months, I was ready for the next move and was looking to go back to marketing or project management. I was offered a promotion in procurement. I did not take the bigger role and money because my job was done there, and I had absolutely demonstrated the capabilities and skills that I needed for my career in that role.

Later in my career, another critical development decision moved me into my first in-line brand job for the company. I was there to build another set of capabilities. I was a year into the role when the company decided to undertake a significant business model redesign to take out millions of dollars in costs. My name was put forth because of an earlier experience I had in bringing two companies together.

I was honored to be asked, but did not want to leave the line job unless my sponsors thought I had successfully demonstrated the skills that we agreed on for this role. I was specific about the ask.

**"Have I demonstrated running the in-line brand job in the complexities of the US market for this billion-dollar brand? If the answer is yes, I will move on, but if the answer is no, I don't want to come back to check this box." The answer was no, and so I stayed for eight more months to put the win on this part of my résumé.**

## There is no better time to power up than with the opportunity to move into a new role.

When you move into a new role, there is a lot coming at you all at once. Perhaps it's a role in a different function, or a different country. Maybe you are moving into general management from a functional role, and running a P&L with all new challenges. Maybe you got promoted, and now your peers report to you.

As you read the stories of the leaders represented in this book, the wisdom learned through hard lessons comes powering through. It has been said,

"Learn from the mistakes of others. You can't live long enough to make them all yourself."

So, here are a few mistakes that our Wisdom Warriors share so you don't have to make them.

## Mistake #1
### Get in and immediately strive to prove yourself.

*NO:* Focus first on the people, not the work. While it is human nature to want to prove yourself in the new role, remember that you were given this role because you earned it. Now that you are there,

the last thing you want to do is to immediately make decisions and changes. You can't know it all, and you don't need to. Build relationships with your new stakeholders. Get to know the capabilities of your team because the ability to take on a bigger role means building capacity. Surrounding yourself with great talent, better than yourself, can give you that capacity. This is also the time for active listening. Learn before you decide.

Sarena Lin moved from leading strategy at Cargill to running the entire animal nutrition business as President, Cargill Feed & Nutrition (see Sarena's story on page 124).

**"All of a sudden I went from running a group of 90 smart strategists to 15,000 people around the globe. My boss reminded me that I was there to empower the team so they can do their best. I spent a lot of time learning and listening, and eventually I gave myself permission to lead from the front."**

## Mistake #2
### Give space to a former peer who becomes your direct report.

*NO:* Tackle the delicate relationships early. When a colleague has lost out on the position because you got it, relationships can become strained. It's much better to put the elephant in the room and address the situation head on, *but with care*. Maria Blasé experienced this when she moved from the regional CFO job to President of HVAC and Transport, Latin America for Ingersoll Rand (see Maria's story on page 146).

"The worst thing you can do is to avoid them and not have that unspoken conversation about your new working relationship. With the right kind of discussion, your promotion doesn't necessarily have to be a problem at all. Make sure that you understand what that person wants from their career and their timing. Make sure that they know that you're in their corner to help them achieve whatever they want to achieve. In most cases, people will give you time to demonstrate your commitment to sponsoring their development."

# Reshaping My Leadership Brand

I recently moved to a new position inside the company that required far wider stakeholder management with a lot of people that I didn't yet know. I had to be very deliberate about keeping to my brand while I observed, absorbed, and learned. My brand preceded me in this role, which in most cases was good, but I also have a reputation for being too aggressive at times, fast paced, and sometimes impatient. I am sure people were waiting for me to just start pushing things forward, and it took a lot of self-restraint to not jump right in.

**Shereen Zarkani**
**Global Head of Reefer Management | Maersk Line**

# Mistake #3
## Act like you always have; it got you here.

*NO:* Moving into a new position is the perfect opportunity to reposition your leadership brand or evolve it for a different kind of role. One of the first things you can do is gain a solid understanding of how you are perceived. I like to focus on one key question to ask with your new team and sponsors: "What are my unique differences relative to others who have had this role?"

It provides instant awareness for you, and the person giving you the response, that you are indeed different from your predecessor and likely to have a different approach than what they are used to. It also tells you how you are initially perceived. This creates the opportunity to consciously amend or strengthen your leadership brand the way you want. Thinking about how you show up is critically important to managing how you are perceived.

When Frances Franken-Mulder, General Manager of Gall & Gall B.V., a division of Ahold Delhaize, moved into her first GM role, it required a huge transformation. The very skills that got her that job were needed, such as drive, energy, and innovation. But her reputation of not listening enough could have derailed her, if she wasn't careful. Her boss gave her great advice.

**"Keep your mouth shut for the first three months. Just ask; don't give your opinion."**

It was very hard at first, but she had terrific outcomes for both the business and for herself (see Frances's story on page 78).

# Mistake #4
## Roll your sleeves up and start changing lots of things.

*NO:* The desire to deliver results quickly can create the syndrome of "death by too many initiatives." You will want to immediately demonstrate how you will enact positive change, but trying to do too many things at once will ensure that you underdeliver on many of them.

Amanda Montgomery, VP of Industrial Bearings at The Timken Company, explains that you need to pay attention to both the task agenda and the people agenda.

*"Early in your career, success is usually defined as results, which tend to be very task-oriented. What are the things you got done? But as you move into a leadership role, you need to balance the task agenda with the people agenda. If you're only getting things done, with no attention to the people side of things, or all the attention is on people, but you aren't delivering the results, neither is going to be successful long-term. Whether it's leading a meeting, assigning projects, or working with someone one-on-one, it can be difficult to balance the needs of the people when you are so used to driving the task. But doing so will set you apart at the higher leadership levels."*

# Mistake #5

## Jump in full-force and invest lots of hours to come up to speed fast.

*NO:* Let's face it, that early part of a new role is usually super intense. We always seem to put in more hours, skip meals, lose our workout routine, and see family less, vowing that it's just "for now." The mistake most people make is to overextend themselves and not take care of their health and energy needs. Capacity is all about "YOU" management. This is the very time you should NOT overload. Creating energy for yourself helps you get through those first 100 days and the days to come after that. **Think of it as still drinking from the fire hose, but making sure you wear protective rain gear.** This is also the time to think about *relationships first*, then the job second.

Anda Cristescu, Global Operations Director, Cargill Ocean Transportation of Cargill, reflects on her learnings when navigating the first 100 days of a new role. Number one on her list is about the relationship.

"Before I start another new job, I make a plan as to what areas I need to look at from a business perspective and from a people perspective. What things, individuals, and dynamics do I need to focus on? Whose inputs should I take advantage of? I'm be very mindful of four things during the first three months:

✓ Who I spend time with
✓ What areas I involve myself in
✓ What types of decisions I make
✓ What image I create

**After all, you don't get a second chance for a first impression. So, be yourself."**

---

# It's All About Pacing

*Being in the C-suite, it is much easier for me to manage my time. It's not that I work fewer hours. It's that I'm managing what I work on, and I have some flexibility. You know how to get done what needs to be done. Take time to think it through so you don't kill it, yourself, and other people.*

*When I was new at Hertz, I drove myself crazy working Saturdays and Sundays. I knew it wasn't sustainable. I looked at my to-do list and thought, "I'm putting stuff on here because I know what really good HR is, and I have this driving need to deliver what I think employees deserve. But I'm going to kill myself and my team if I don't take some of this off. Let's pace this." So I gave myself a let and took control of my calendar.*

**LeighAnne Baker**
Corporate SVP and Chief Human Resources Officer | Cargill

# Frances Franken-Mulder

## I like to win, but not on my own. Together, it's more fun.

I firmly believe that you always should communicate your wishes. They might come true. **How will they know if you don't tell them?**

When I took the role, my boss gave me the best advice, "Keep your mouth shut for the first three months. Just ask; don't give your opinion." My reputation was that I had lots of drive, lots of energy, innovation and vision, but that I didn't listen enough or give people space.

When he introduced me, he said,

**"This is Frances, and she's going to continue the strategy of the predecessor." Everything in me yelled, "No! I'm not going to! This company needs to turn around!"**

But I didn't speak up. I had to force myself to be more open-minded. If you listen to other sources, especially outside the company, you can learn a lot. And it makes you humble.

So I kept on asking questions, listening for views and ideas. We came up with the "Next Phase" strategy. Eventually it will become a clear different strategy, but for now I want to make sure that the company that was started in 1884 can successfully continue for the next hundred years. I want to give the company a good future perspective, just as the founder of our company, Mrs. Maria Gall, had in mind back in 1884.

*FRANCES*

I like selling stuff to people and have been doing it all my life. I started by building a business selling university merchandise. All the students wanted the sweaters and sports gear, and competition backed off. That's how it all started.

At 21, I started with Procter & Gamble in account management selling detergents. I liked it because I was able to work with a team of people to sell even more stuff than other companies could. I think I liked the game of it. P&G taught me to be fact-based.

I always had a General Manager job on my wish list. The Ahold leaders knew it and the call came two and a half years ago. I love it every day.

*Frances is the General Manager of Gall & Gall B.V.*

# Q
## What is different about being in the C-suite?

**Jane Leipold:** You have to be a steward of that company's assets and help strategically point the direction for the company. The top jobs really require vision and being able to see ambiguity and dealing with paradox. It's a big jump from having a piece of the company to understanding all the complex internal and external factors at play, each and every day.

—Jane Leipold, retired SVP Human Resources | TE Connectivity

**Lucien Alziari:** The one thing that is the most enjoyable (and the thing most people don't get) is that now you're a member of the company's leadership team — and that's more important than being a functional leader. The biggest contribution you have to make now is to how the whole business wins. That's a bigger job than running a function. It's assumed that you're going to do that. You have to add something to the leadership team of the company; otherwise, you are not really needed.

—Lucien Alziari, Chief Human Resources Officer | Maersk Group

**Joanne Bauer:** I had been in charge of one of the floor operating units at Kimberly-Clark. When I moved into the C-suite, I had to reconcile to that team that I was no longer just thinking about them. They had to understand that decisions have to be made for the benefit of the business. Another thing I had to factor in was all those people that you're fairly removed from, even at a vice-president level, become big players. All of a sudden, you really become cognizant of your Wall Street investors.

—Joanne Bauer, retired President Health Care | Kimberly-Clark Corporation

**Teri McClure:** It is thinking about issues that are beyond just your functional expertise. You have to understand that the expectation is at that level that you're there to give your broad-based experience and perspective on very wide-ranging issues that aren't just legal, or aren't just HR, or aren't just marketing. We work very collaboratively at the senior levels, and we are expected to be able to contribute in all areas.

—Teri McClure, Chief Human Resources Officer and SVP Labor Relations | United Parcel Service of America, Inc.

**Pam Kimmet:** I think one of the differentiators — whether it's a man or a woman — that takes somebody all the way to a C-suite level position is they really want it for the right reasons. The real driving force for wanting to be in, and making it to a top seat, is believing in yourself and wanting the role because it enables you to have greater impact and to make a positive difference. You will have many people, and very accomplished ones, working for you, but you have to still put forth the effort and earn that role every day. It requires you to constantly learn and assimilate lots of things to determine how to take your team and company forward. That takes a high level of devotion because it needs to be embedded in the very fabric of who you are. It is a full-time commitment, but that is okay, because you really love what you do!

—Pam Kimmet, Chief Human Resources Officer | Cardinal Health

## The Gift of Feedback

It used to be that feedback for the job came in an annual performance review. In one 60-minute sitting, you would get your entire year's worth of feedback. If you heard "you are doing great," you would smile, sigh with relief, and the conversation might turn to what's ahead for the career, or it might just go to pleasantries (*whew*, we are done with that!). That equated to a missed opportunity to have meaningful conversations about your course of action and potential for growth.

Wisdom Warriors in this book are taking more action to ask for feedback and give feedback. They are doing this with more frequency and higher quality. One of the executives described that getting feedback was a "gift," and she made a pact with her boss to get it often, sometimes daily.

The key is to remind yourself that feedback is about the business and not about you. Conversations about raises, responsibilities, reporting relationships, and decision-making authority will be more progressive if you can depersonalize it.

Joanne Bauer used a unique approach on feedback to change the entire culture of her organization. As the new President of the Kimberly-Clark Health Care Division, she made active and honest feedback a key tenet of the change agenda, and her leaders needed to model the behavior. Joanne did this daily and said the key to success was demonstrating she would act on the feedback (read Joanne's story on page 164).

## How You Receive Feedback is Just as Important as How You Give It

One day, our CEO called me up and said, "A few months ago, you asked me what your brand is and now I want to give you some feedback." He paused and then went on. "You've more than ruffled feathers. You're intense about getting things done. You put together top teams, and you get results, but you have to be careful not to alienate people." I responded "Yeah, you're right. I know I've got some things to work on."

**You can't negotiate your brand or your reputation. But you can work on it daily.**

Your bad habits can be derailers, regardless of where you are in your career. Whatever makes you successful can also take you out. However, by admitting what things I needed to be conscious of and working on them, I got to where I am today. I was truly honored when our CEO asked me to join his new 10-person executive team after that conversation.

**Kathy Fortmann**
President, Cargill Business Services | Cargill

## Getting Good Performance Feedback? Now Ask the Real Questions.

Things are going very well in your performance review. Everything is "fine" and you are doing "well." Then a year down the road, things aren't so fine, and you are not being promoted. Take this opportunity to ask the real questions. "What does my career path look like? Could you see me in this job? Could you see me in another job?" Sometimes the opportunity will come outside of a performance review. When you finish a big project, go and ask, "How could I have done this better?" Or when there is an issue, suggest, "Let's talk about how we might approach this in a different way."

**Ronee Hagen**
Retired President & CEO | Polymer Group, Inc.

# The Power of Three Things

A decade ago, Lucien Alziari, now Chief Human Resources Officer for Maersk Group, and I were teaching a class of "next CHROs." I recalled the power of one of his ideas, and I have been using this wisdom for myself and others, ever since.

"When you're in an executive role, sometimes you need to 'unlearn' to be successful. You are no longer playing a volume game. You won't succeed based upon the number of initiatives you drive. Five years from now, you are only going to be remembered for three things. Organizations can't remember more than three things. So think really hard about what you want those things to be and what you want people to remember you for.

Choose the three things you think will really matter for the business. Do you know enough about your business that you can find the right three things for the business? Consider whether you are dealing with substantive issues and underlying causes, or if you're dealing with symptoms. Good for you that you have figured it out. But do you have the communication and alignment skills to get everybody else to sign up for it? Not only that, do you also have the stamina and the drive for results to spend 80% of your time on those three things for the next three to five years?"

For any leadership role, you need to strike a point of view about how you are going to "win" in your business. It's not just about the area for which you have responsibility, but how it fits into the enterprise.

Articulate the three things you will focus on to drive impact for the business. Then, be sure to always begin your conversations with, "These are the three things we said we would put the most time and energy into for the benefit of the business. Since we last spoke, here is how the team is advancing each of these three things." If you keep communicating this, you can create clarity in the organization about priority, and it will be easier to say "no" to things that don't fit with those three imperatives.

# Sandra Beach Lin

*For me, curiosity is an essential leadership trait. It has led me to seek a variety of experiences, which is a huge source of my energy.*

"We knew you would do things that we had never done" were my father's words to me. Ever since my Junior Achievement days in high school, I've known I wanted to have a career in business. That experience flipped a switch inside of me. Junior Achievement taught me about business, competition, and leadership. And it helped me visualize doing different things that hadn't been the standard in our family, like getting a college degree and taking an overseas assignment.

That first foreign assignment was pivotal for my career. My husband and I had just built our dream home in Cleveland, Ohio, when I got a job offer to move to Singapore with Allied Signal. That opportunity turned out to be a great role; a broadening experience that was an enormous accelerator for my career. My exposure to the CEO was much greater there because I was among just a handful of expats, and the only female. It was a growth experience for the whole family, as our children got to experience many Asian cultures.

*Sandra is a Board Member for American Electric Power, PolyOne, WESCO, and Interface Biologics*

### Stepping into that overseas assignment taught me the value of being "maze bright."

For me, being "maze bright," a term originally coined by Ronee Hagen as she traveled up the corporate ladder, involves two skills. First, reading the maze of players in your organization. What roles do each of them play now? What roles do they want to play? What makes each of them tick? What do they really think? And second, figuring out how you succeed within that maze of personalities, priorities, and power in a rapidly changing world. What is changing? What does that mean in terms of your company, your business, your division?

**Whenever I transition to a new role, I listen.** For the first 90 to 100 days, I talk with employees, customers, investors, and shareholders. I listen to learn and to discover what I need to master for the larger role I'm taking on. With my first large VP/GM job, for instance, the level of ambiguity, not surprisingly, increased significantly. Dealing with ambiguity became a focus area for me that first year.

When I became the CEO of a startup, where there was rapid change on a daily basis, I learned to utilize leadership team meetings as a way to, not only make sure that I was hearing what was going on everywhere in the business, but also to ensure that the entire team was hearing what was going on with our customers, our financial results, and our people, on a frequent basis. More than information-sharing, we shared the bigger picture of where we were taking the company, how we would manage talent, and how best to execute. **Dealing with ambiguity became a team skill during these dynamic times.**

## Safety is a Non-Negotiable

Whatever business you are in, but especially if you are in industrial companies as I have been in, you can discern quickly its culture by how they approach safety. I'm very serious about safety and care deeply that people go home from work in the same condition that they came in. For me, safety is the foundation of a company's strength.

That means I'm as likely to call a timeout when a safety-related incident occurs in a plant as I am to make sure my Uber driver is wearing his/her seat belt. Great companies use many tools, like holding town halls for all shifts in a manufacturing facility where the leadership can discuss how critically we view safety, to send the right message. These firms then involve the people who are there every day to come up with ideas for improvement. A company with a strong safety culture knows that "zero incidents" is possible.

### I believe in continuous improvement, wholeheartedly. My curious nature keeps me growing and learning and relevant. Much of that learning comes from listening.

The variety of boards I choose to be on reflects my curiosity. They're not all in the same field, so I'm constantly reading new materials and attending relevant industry events about corporate governance, technology, talent, and workforce management. All of these inputs help me stay current, see how trends in one area can impact others, and bring fresh thinking to the companies whose boards I sit on.

My curiosity and my passion for leaving a legacy are taking my voice outside the boardroom, as well. The variety I place in my life, whether it's serving on the local board of the National Association of Corporate Directors, the executive board of my national sorority, or with the Paradigm for Parity℠ movement for gender parity in corporations, fuels my energy.

*Nancy*

### Ask for It

Powering up in your life and career can come down to something so simple, and yet feel so hard.

**We need to ask for broader roles or different roles that fit our gift zone. We need to ask for the title and the money if we are moving into expanded roles, as well the "authority" to make the decisions. We need to ask for help both at work and at home.**

### Put that intentional mindset to work for you.

One of our graduates did just this after the program. She decided that she had been in emerging countries too long and wanted to play a commercial role in a developed market. She found an opportunity on her company postings and crafted a new résumé that articulated her leadership brand, her passions, her gifts, and her intentions to help grow that business. She went through numerous interviews, always stating her intentions. All interviews went well as she progressed through the process, and she was awaiting the job offer on a Friday afternoon.

# Put Your Aspirations Out There!

If you have an aspiration, put it out there. This is your career, so own it. Be clear about what you want. And then ask for it.

Your career conversation needs to be specific. Doing "whatever is best for the company" won't get you there. If that's where your conversation stops, the boss is going to give the role to someone who is much more purposeful. You need to describe what your aspiration looks like, what the role or job is that you want. The more concrete and specific you can make your description, the greater your chances that the organization will find it for you. No company can meet everyone's aspirations, but every company can know what everyone's aspirations are.

**If you don't tell us what you want, how on earth will we know?**

**Lucien Alziari**
**Chief Human Resources Officer | Maersk Group**

You've got to move to where the opportunities are. You have to be willing to say, "I'm not going to hit my goals here," and just take your toys and go play someplace else.

**LeighAnne Baker**

Corporate SVP and Chief Human Resources Officer | Cargill

---

Then the President called her. He said,

**"Lauren, you have been very articulate about your intentions for the business and the value you can bring. You have communicated your brand and your passion. You have the job, but I am going to ask you to turn this role down. I have something else in mind for you, and it will be a win/win for the business."**

Lauren was intentional about asking for a role that fit her passions and her strengths by articulating what she stood for and how she could add value to the business. As a result, she was offered an even better role than the one she posted for, and she and the business both benefited.

## Crafting Your Own Role

I started this chapter sharing that I had been unemployed for 11 months. I had a job offer that was a fit for my values. I really liked the other Executive Team members I would collaborate with, and in particular, the CEO and the Chairman.

But the job did not pass my filter as a growth role. It was a more traditional CMO position. **So I decided to change the shape of the role and ask for something I wanted.** I went out to the market and did a "360 review" on the company. I interviewed competitors, buyers of their services, and even the CEO of the industry association they belonged to. I gathered their perspectives of the company. I created a one-page circle of quotes from those outside perspectives which were more powerful than my opinion. Then I created my value proposition, drawing on my unique gifts, I articulated the difference I could make to this organization. The Chairman and CEO now saw this role as creating enterprise value, rather than the more functionally-focused CMO role they had envisioned. I was named Chief Commercial Officer, and built and led an entirely new product development team to drive growth (along with owning the traditional CMO duties). This put me smack in the center of my gift zone. I was energized, passionate, and had the capacity to deliver on the value I pitched coming into the company.

# Teri McClure

## *I have been very intentional about my brand.*

Our company has a process of "learn as you go," as well as formalized development plans. You get the opportunity to learn in the job, which is scary in some respects, but for me it created great opportunities because there were no limitations. I can't honestly say that I felt completely ready, or equipped to handle any job they moved me to, but the company was gracious enough to give me time to grow into it and to trust me.

### "You went to law school to go work in a garage?"

At one point in my career, I was asked to step out of the legal department to run a pickup and delivery operation in central Florida. My manager told me that if I wanted to go further in the organization, I had to understand the business and actually work in the operations. This was a tough family decision, as we had to relocate and my husband had a business. I was leaving the role as head of labor and employment, with no promises of a promotion. With no operational experience, and as a black female running a trucking operation, it was a huge stretch and huge personal growth.

I was told it was going to be for a certain period of time. That period of time ended, and all the people who had talked to me about the move were gone. They retired, they moved on, so I had lost my advocates and support. "Okay, I'm ready to come

*Teri is the Chief Human Resources Officer and SVP, Labor Relations at United Parcel Service of America, Inc.*

back now. I've gotten my experience. I'm ready to come back." The response was, "We don't have a job for you." My husband and I had made this deal for a certain time period, and the time was up. The company said, "We'll move you back, but we don't have a job for you."

I literally sat in an office and was on "special assignment." I just kept my faith and said I'm not going to rush and jump at something just because I'm not comfortable where I am right now. Ultimately, things turned out, and the experience set me up for the General Counsel role.

### 'Why aren't they doing that? They're too slow to do this.' Then when you take it over, it's, 'Oh, okay, I get it now. It's not as simple as it looks on the outside.'

When I took my current position, I remember first standing on the outside, looking in, and observing what those groups were doing, and in some respects being very critical. "Man, why aren't they doing this?" You really don't understand the complexities of a given situation or the limitations that they're facing. Sometimes we are quick to judge. In the top role, you have to be patient enough to go in and uncover the layers of complexity, and understand the barriers to success — what's keeping the function, or the business unit, or the organization from being able to operate as you think it should. Having a critical eye from the outside and looking in, you realize you don't appreciate everything that they're doing.

### You can't have anyone else define your boundaries for you. You have to define them for yourself.

While I've been very driven most of my career, I've also had very firm boundaries in terms of our personal family choices, my faith, my desire to do things outside of the company, and my commitment to the community. I am very clear on how I want to work, the type of company I want to work in, where I want to live, and how I want to interact with my family. All of my decisions reside within those boundaries. And I have been very intentional about my brand. In many respects, that's allowed me to be very successful.

I could have job-jumped a thousand times, but I may not have had an environment where I could pursue both my social and civic interests, as well as my corporate interest, and still do that in a very meaningful way. I happen to work for a company that allows me to do that.

---

# A Better Way to Open Doors

When I was first starting out at the company, an experienced manager told me, "If you want to get to know the people that you're going to be working with, just go and make an appointment. Sit down and talk with them. People love to talk about themselves." No matter what new job I go into, that is the first thing I now do. I map out the influencers, the people I'm going to need to have on my side, and the people I'm going to be working for.

Then I just make it a point to go in, sit down, and get to know them. I often start the conversation with, "What can I do for you? What do you need help with? How has this role been helpful to you in the past? How has it not been helpful to you?" It tends to break the ice and lets people know that you're there to help them, not undermine their world. That seems to have helped open doors for me.

---

# Tina Tromiczak

*I had to learn to accept what I would not be.*

But I was going into operations, so I started to try to learn everything the folks were doing.

**I remember my boss telling me, "I don't want you to do it. I've got people to do it. I want you to lead it."**

That was probably one of the best pieces of advice I ever got. As my roles and responsibilities increased and the industries I worked in changed, I would have never been able to keep up. I don't believe you ever fully learn the work that you lead. You ask question after question after question. And you change the way people think.

I've always felt like a leader and thought I could run anything. That is, until I got more involved in the sales side of the business. I didn't like it. I was uncomfortable and awkward. I was trying to work on things I wasn't good at. I didn't fit.

I get excited about figuring out how to improve a process or the product for the client, how to mentor and coach people coming up through the ranks, how to make things happen that we don't think we possibly can. I love that! I love the frustration, the challenge of service and operations. So now I know I will never run sales because that is not who I am.

Actually, there are a lot of things I now know that I won't be. I learned I don't have a fear that I'll not be good at something I *want* to do. I believe you figure it out as you go. You know that research that says men will look at jobs and not have half of the experience, and they will still go for it? Well, I will, too.

I fix things. That's who I am. The more broken, the more chaos, the harder I work to fix it!

I think it comes from my parents. I have a work standard that might make some folks crazy. Growing up, my parents gave every minute of every day to the schools they taught in, to the kids they coached and taught, to the community we lived in, and to our church. Those values, and being involved in the community, were deeply instilled in me. I can't sit still. I'm always doing something.

Those values morphed into needing new and bigger challenges. The unknown and the uncomfortable drive me. I wanted to be in the business. I wanted to lead people and I wanted to win. When I first went into manufacturing, my expertise and skills at that time were in human resources.

*Tina is the SVP, Global Business Solutions of ADP*

# Advice to My Younger Self

## Career Momentum

**Spend the time to really figure out what you want.**

Not what you think management wants you to want. Not what you think you should want to position yourself well politically. But what you truly want. And then put that forward in your development plans. Anything less than that truth will hinder your career.

When you get real and can articulate what you want in a way that is authentic to you, your career will gain much more momentum. You will be much better able to know which things to turn down and which to accept, which things to prioritize and which to discard — and you can do all of that with a lot less guilt.

### Maria Blasé
**President of HVAC and Transport, Latin America | Ingersoll Rand**

"You yourself, as much as anybody in the entire universe, deserve your love and affection."

— Proverb

# Peace

I was on an executive team charged with turning around a company to make it a viable business again. Though I had passion and energy for this challenge, the pace was relentless. I didn't sit down. **I didn't stop to think. I didn't stop to reflect, or breathe, or wonder.** Suddenly I started to have health issues.

*An MRI didn't show any issues*, so physical therapy was recommended. Months went by. Nothing seemed to work. I tried chiropractic, massage therapy, and acupuncture. I got relief for a while. One day, as I was speaking with my physical therapist about the nagging problem, he said I needed to practice more "self-care." Frankly, I had not heard the term before, but I figured, logically, that it had to do with taking care of my physical self. He expanded that to say it included taking care of myself emotionally, mentally, and spiritually. When I got home later, I went straight to the computer and Googled it.

And here is how Wikipedia defined it:

---

# Self-Care *(noun)*

1. How you treat yourself is how you invite the world to treat you.

Wow. The pace I had set was self-inflicted. And as I demonstrated that behavior, others thought it was okay for me, too. I had chosen that behavior, of course. But that was the problem — or, rather, the solution.

## It was my choice.

Self-care? Now I get it. Food. Sleep. Movement. Stretch. Rest. *Recovery.*

But it also means letting go. Setting limits. Taking time to breathe, reflect, dream, and wonder. Living in peace. I needed to understand and buy into peace, so that I could help heal myself.

I learned that the only person who really could take care of me was me. If I continued to try and muscle through all the projects and commitments without taking time for myself, or letting others help, I would continue to spiral downward.

# Perspective and Priorities

I probably wouldn't have said this when I was coming back from maternity leave after my first child. Having been through this three times now, I've had a little bit of practice. I now realize that having children has been quite empowering to me. Pre-children, I was really burning the candle at both ends. I realized post-children that I couldn't afford to do that anymore. Not just because I wanted to spend time with my children, but because I was actually running myself into the ground.

I had to figure out a better way to bring my work life and my personal life together. I first focused on physical resiliency; getting sleep, eating well, and having fun. That made me better in the workplace. I was bringing a better self to work. I was better able to cope with the stresses that were thrown at me. Having children also made me reflect about priorities. It's about not being afraid to weed out what is truly important versus what everyone else is telling you is important.

### Shanna Wendt
#### VP of Communications | Coca-Cola European Partners

## Work-Life FLEX

I don't believe in work-life balance, because balance implies stasis. For me, it is much more about flexing. It's setting boundaries and making commitments to both sides of your life. It's flexing one way or the other and understanding that sometimes your life is going to be higher focused on work, sometimes higher focused on family. I feel very fortunate that throughout most of my career I've worked for organizations that understand how important my family is to me. And I have a family who understands how important my work is to me.

Importantly, too, I try to approach both my personal and professional lives with a healthy dose of humor and perspective. If I'm not having at least one shared laugh or smile during a call or meeting, I'm not going to enjoy that experience. That's not going to be the place for me where I'm going to thrive. I'm darn serious about the work, but I really want to have a little fun along the way.

I care desperately about the business. But I'm far calmer about the business stuff than I am with what happens to my family.

### Kathryn Beiser
Global Chair, Corporate Practice | Edelman

# Work-Life Balance: Is There Such a Thing?

If I were to play word association with someone in the business world, the most likely reaction I would receive to a prompt of "self-care" would be "work-life balance," but I have never, ever liked this term. It implies a trade-off.

How do you do it all? That question is often asked of the leaders in Wisdom Warriors. I should not have been surprised to find that the executives in this book don't relate to the term "work-life balance," either. Not because they work too much, but because they don't see their lives as separate parts.

**They blend WORK and FAMILY into ONE life. INTENTIONALLY.**

# Cathy Doherty

*There can only be one calendar. It's a calendar for life that includes work and life. There's not two; it's all one.*

You create balance in the long term, not daily, just like relationships are not a daily balance. Sometimes you have to give more; sometimes you're taking more. I think work is similar. Sometimes you're peaking at work and valleying with your family. Sometimes you're peaking with your family and valleying at work. In that process, you need to understand what your priorities are so that you can create balance and create value in the long term, like most relationships.

**I am a very forward thinker and a planner, but it's not obsessive. I live in the present, but I also think about the future.**

My career choices have been a balancing act between two commitments: one to family, and one to learning and growth. I started out as a CPA, working with KPMG across many industries. When Adidas USA, my client, offered me a job I couldn't refuse, I was engaged to be married and still living at home. At that time, you typically doubled your salary when you moved from public accounting to a private corporation. My parents said, "Oh, my God. You took it,

*Cathy is the SVP & Group Executive, Clinical Franchise Solutions of Quest Diagnostics*

right?" I said, "Well, no. I'm going to think about it because I want to make sure that this is the environment that I want to be in, an environment I'm going to learn and grow in." They were astonished I didn't just go for it. But I was thinking further ahead than the offer that was right in front of me.

## I didn't want financial gain to be the driving force behind my next career decision.

Marriage and family were also on my mind. I wanted my husband-to-be to come into our marriage with his eyes wide open. So before we got engaged, I'd talk through scenarios with him. Imagine if I have a dinner meeting one evening. Or what if I am not the one cooking or doing the laundry in the relationship? We talked about the possibility that there might even come a time when one person's career might take precedence over the other's. We didn't need to solve that problem yet, but we needed to know that we both would be open to solving it together, if and when that happened.

One problem I did have to solve in the present, though, was my work location. I was spending, at least, 90 minutes every day traveling to and from work. I knew that my work location would have an even more significant impact on my life when we started our family. It was time to find another opportunity closer to home.

Metpath, the predecessor to Quest Diagnostics, offered me a job as Manager of Corporate Accounting — but with a 10% pay cut. Many people told me not to take the offer, and that if I considered the compounded impact on my lifetime earnings, it was a no-brainer. However, **decisions are not black and white. There's an awful lot of grey matter that needs to be considered.** I made the decision to take the job, and not only did I make up the pay cut within six months through a special bonus, but I have been here for 26 years now, rising to a senior vice president role. It was clearly the right move, pay cut and all.

## Although I felt valued in the organization, I wasn't certain I was being seen as adding value, separate from my boss.

In 1999, after being at Quest for nine years, Quest acquired SmithKline Beecham Clinical Laboratories, our largest competitor. So I went to my boss and said, "I've really enjoyed working for you. I've learned a ton. But I'm not sure the organization knows whether I'm all that valuable because they only see me through you. Now that the company has doubled in size, I think it's the perfect time for me to explore other opportunities." His response was fantastic. "That's right. What can I do to help you?" He immediately discussed the recent decision to put a dedicated Investor Relations role in place. I had been doing a lot of work with the analysts since the company had gone public. I said I was interested in the position, but unfortunately, not if it reported to him. Twenty-four hours later, my boss came back and asked, "What if the job reports to our CEO?" Although that wasn't what I had in mind, it was the move that was the catalyst for my career progression.

# Amanda Montgomery

*My parents always told me, "You can do anything you want to do." What I heard, but they never said, was "I can do everything."*

A lot of times I get asked, "How do you do it all?" My answer is, "I don't." It took me a while to get comfortable with that. I am extremely thankful that I had parents who constantly reinforced that I could do anything. But anything is not everything. There are things I have to rely on others to do for me. There are support networks — family, friends, colleagues, mentors — I've had to put in place.

My father was an athletic director, and I was very engaged in sports as I was growing up. I didn't like it at

*Amanda is the VP, Industrial Bearings of The Timken Company*

the time, but I learned I had to listen to my coach and accept that he got to make the calls, even if I didn't agree. I learned a lot, and I know it has helped me accept feedback in my job and be comfortable with being coached.

## Spend Your Time Where You Know the Least

I've learned that I have to choose where I spend my time. When I took on my current role, it was the first time I was responsible for an area of the business where I not only did not have expertise, but I also had to lead a team where I was not the functional knowledge expert.

My coach gave me some great advice on choosing where I spend my time — where I know the least!

It's most people's natural tendency to focus on what we know versus what we don't know, particularly early in a new role when we are trying to create credibility. But **you can come in quickly at any time on a white horse to help "save the day" in the area you already know. Your team needs you to invest your time in the new areas.**

*Amanda*

# How do you make work-life balance work for you?

**Sarena Lin:** I only have one life. Work is part of my life. It's one pie, and I divide it differently based on what I need to deal with at the moment.

—Sarena Lin, President, Feed & Nutrition | Cargill

**Teri McClure:** I have very firm boundaries in terms of my personal family choices, my faith, my desire to do things outside of the company, and my commitment to the community. I am very clear on how I want to work, the type of company I want to work in, where I want to live, and how I want to interact with my family. All of my decisions reside within those boundaries.

—Teri McClure, Chief Human Resources Officer and SVP of Labor Relations | United Parcel Service of America, Inc.

**Julie Fasone Holder:** I actually call it shades of grey because I think what happens with women is we often get in this "all-or-nothing" thought process. Realize that every day you're making tradeoffs, and you're not going to be a horrible mom because you missed this particular event.

What really happens in life is you miss one event, but you make the next. You have to think about the choices you make as "this is the choice for today." This is not a choice for the rest of your life. And learn to live with the guilt! If I'm at home, I'm guilty I'm not at work. When I'm at work, I'm guilty I'm not at home.

—Julie Fasone Holder, CEO and Founder | JFH Insights

**Kathy Fortmann:** My philosophy has always been very simple: work hard, play hard, and enjoy the journey. I don't think about "balance." I once had a CEO tell me, "You're not very balanced," and I simply replied, "I never said I was." People who know me would say I take the same approach whether I'm doing something for fun or doing something for work, and that is to go all in. What sustains me and what is really important is daily fitness; it is my sanity.

—Kathy Fortmann, President, Cargill Business Services | Cargill

# It's All about Energy!

Managing commitments to work and family requires lots of personal capacity, and capacity is fueled by energy. Leaders need to be able to give energy to those around them. Creating energy, managing your stores of energy, and pacing it throughout the day so you have it when you need it; that's critical.

**You need to have energy left when you go home to your family.**

You can't be successful in these extreme jobs that run at high speed, in technology-assaulted environments, without having a way to create it and sustain it.

## *Bring Your Best Self to Every Situation*

I was turned on years ago to the concept of personal sustainability when I met Scott Peltin, CEO of Tignum.[1]

Tignum trains thousands of executives on creating more capacity so they can take on new challenges, increase their potential for growth and learning, and improve their performance. Tignum explains that in athletics capacity is built progressively through training and practice. In the business world, however, capacity is built on the integration of four key components:

Mindset, Nutrition, Movement, and Recovery, which together create energy throughout our days so that we can perform at our best and sustain that performance.[2] I value our work with the Tignum coaches and their approach on creating sustainable performance. These four key pillars all need to be working together, but small changes implemented using simple strategies can create significant impact on our daily creation of energy.

Preparing for critical events or presentations takes more than putting the content together on the slides. In our chapter on Authenticity, we noted the importance of spending time thinking about how you want to be perceived during and after the presentation. The perception with which you want to leave the audience needs to be visualized and set in your mind. You also need the stamina when you walk into the room to present yourself with energy. Proper movement and recovery techniques, including stretching and sleep, help you prepare for the day and complement your high-performance nutrition. You would not see a world-class athlete grab a candy bar and soft drink on the way to the French Open final. Business executives also need to fuel themselves for peak performance.

Our executives in the program have incorporated many of the strategies with astounding outcomes.

"When I was 30, I thought the scarcest resource was money. When I was 40, I thought the scarcest resource was time. Now that I'm more than 60, I know the scarcest resource is energy."

Sandy Ogg
CEO.works

# How to Create Sustainable High Performance — *By Design*

## High-Performance Mindset

✓ Articulate clear intentions for your desired outcome.

✓ Visualize how you want to be perceived and the emotional state you want to have.

✓ Reflect on your performance. Focus on the things that went right vs. dwelling on what went wrong.

### By Design

*When preparing for a significant presentation, prepare not only the content, but how you want your audience to receive the message and perceive you when you are done.*

## High-Performance Nutrition

✓ Create an energy state to ensure emotional balance and confidence by stabilizing your blood sugar.

✓ Select nutritional needs that enable a good night's sleep.

✓ Hydrate to ensure metabolic function serves mind and body.

### By Design

*Plan for your day to ensure that all systems are operating on all cylinders. Pack or store water and high-energy snacks to use throughout the day, and strategically think about client or entertainment dinner choices before you get to the table.*

## High-Performance Movement

✓ Create an energy system that strengthens mobility, stability, and balance. Movement choices are different than exercise.

✓ Avoid sitting as it contributes to low energy and degenerative conditions.

✓ Utilize morning and evening movement rituals to tune up your energy system.

### By Design

*Plan for stretch or movement every 90 minutes to increase alertness and confidence. When stressed, change locations or take a set of stairs to the next floor. Changing physiology changes your psychology.*

## High-Performance Recovery

✓ Take your foot off the gas to oscillate through deep breathing, stretching, or a power nap.

✓ Use food as a strategic recovery, rather than ignoring hunger and plowing ahead.

### By Design

*Incorporate 15 minutes of unscheduled time two or three times a day. Keeping this free from structure allows for creative thinking; and your physical recovery is enhanced.*

# Andrea Grant

## Anxiety is how it feels to grow.

I am a petite, blonde female, and I didn't have the physical presence or the immediate perceived credibility when I walked into a room with some of my male counterparts. The number of times people thought that I was the P.A. was incredible. Often I've been asked if I was picking up the boss's dry cleaning when it was my own.

I worked, early on, to establish my leadership brand and to be true to myself. The underpinning theory came from the leadership philosopher, Peter Koestenbaum, which anchors into a "leadership brand diamond."[3] On the horizontal axis of my diamond is courage and compassion; the vertical axis is wisdom and joy.

This was quite a risk for joy to be one of my brand values because you don't expect a senior leader to say, "I'm going to be joyous in the workplace." **To give myself permission to be myself, to be happy, to laugh, and be joyful in the workplace was career-changing for me.** It enabled me to have a personality that was my own, and still be highly credible because of it.

I still tell people the story of building my brand and of my struggles during my personal journey. People relate to this vulnerability and see that it's OK for leaders to be human.

A career in human resources can have a major impact on the lives of the employees, their families, and their communities. Work is becoming more of a place where people want to have that sense of belonging. It needs to have a community feel to it. If people come to work and love what they do, they've got friends at work, they feel like they belong, they're developing, growing, and feeling fulfilled, then they go home as a happier partner, parent, sibling, friend, community member.

When I was at both GM and Telstra, the workforces were huge, so the multiplier effect was significant. I think great HR leaders can influence the C-suite to create the right kind of environment in a workplace. It's absolutely the right thing to do for the people who work there, and, of course, it leads to better business outcomes.

*Andrea is the Managing Director of People Ingenuity*

# Getting Ready for My Race Day

## How do we ensure we always turn up to work as our best selves?

I remember hearing an analogy about a Formula One race car. You wouldn't expect to put that car onto the track without it being fully prepared for the race it was about to run. Every race is different. A different track. Different weather conditions. Perhaps a different driver. Different competitors. It really made me think about my life and my work.

## How can I perform my best, every day, in every setting?

Typically, I spend most of my time either traveling or in back-to-back meetings. I'm either interacting face-to-face with people, or on conference calls. A meeting or a call would generally finish on the hour, or a few minutes past the hour, and the next meeting or call would start on the hour. I was always running late! I was never prepared for the next meeting. I would skip lunch and not rehydrate. I would often finish a 10-hour day having purely gone from meeting to meeting, without having achieved much at all. This was typical of most of my peers and had become almost a "company culture."

I wondered how I could change this when the people controlling my diary time were also part of this culture. So I decided to make the change myself and hoped that it might become contagious.

I started booking my meetings to begin at either 10 minutes past the hour, or finish at 10 minutes before the hour. This has caught on with a few of the colleagues with whom I have those meetings. It doesn't happen all of the time, but I can pretty much guarantee now, that in a day of back-to-back meetings, I will have a few 10- to 15-minute gaps. This gives me time to reflect on the last meeting and to stop and think about the next meeting. I can grab a snack and something to drink so that I always show up as my best self. I am more productive.

Jenny Cormack-Lendon

Supply Chain Director, Cargill Agricultural Supply Chain, EMEA | Cargill

# Abbe Luersman

## Finding your footing and then making the right decisions isn't always easy.

My purpose is to create communities that win as one. Personally, I don't like to win alone. That's incredibly boring and not fulfilling to me. I'd much rather achieve things collectively with and through others because the impact is bigger and more fun.

At work I'm evolving organizations, constantly working with different teams to get their buy-in and support, creating a sense of belonging and of being part of something bigger. I'm looking to have the collective group feel like they can win as one, so they really are winning *together*. Outside of work, that purpose plays out as well with my family and friends.

### Challenge is what makes a job exciting. The hard part is pacing yourself when you get excited.

I've always defined myself as someone who's fully on and fully committed. But there's only so much that you can do and only so much that the organization can absorb at once. Weighing these as you're driving change and taking pulse checks along the way are so important to ensure the desired impact.

My current leadership challenge is around the merger of two equals: Ahold and Delhaize. I was blessed to be named CHRO, responsible for the go-forward Ahold Delhaize HR function.

*Abbe is the Chief Human Resources Officer of Ahold Delhaize*

## Give Energy, Get Energy

**I have to have energy to do this work. I know I perform better when the physical, mental, and spiritual all come together.**

Whenever I feel disappointed in my achievements, I can correlate that back to what I've eaten, the exercise I've done, the hours of sleep I've gotten, and the level of engagement I've experienced. I need to eat the right foods and have fun at what I'm doing. I need opportunities for fitness and reflection. I actually need a little more sleep when I'm mentally and physically tired from being pulled in many different directions at once. When I get all these, I'm more resilient and more present, and I can respond faster and make better judgments and decisions. Sometimes I find myself able to be even more caring and giving, even in the midst of a lot of travel and a lot of hours, because I have the reserves to take a more holistic perspective versus funneling in on just the next action to be taken.

## Preparing for the C-suite

When I was preparing to enter the C-suite, I knew I would need to quickly find my footing in a fast-paced environment. I took the opportunity to find out what other people thought of the role I was considering and what they would expect from the person in that role. I really had a desire to be a CHRO, but I also didn't feel ready. During my last year at Unilever, I interviewed more than 20 people who were either current CEOs or CHROs. I asked them what they thought it takes to be a great CHRO, what things to watch out for, and how to define your role on the board.

**Everything I learned through those interviews helped build my confidence that one day, when the right opportunity came up, I could be successful.**

### The Essentials

One thing I can't do without is my running shoes. I'm not a fast runner; I'm a diesel. As I run, I concentrate on taking really deep breaths. Sometimes the moments of intensity in the workday have me running from event to event. To slow myself down, I practice those deep breaths to reset my pace and help me think more clearly. Oh, and every time I go back to the United States, I must have an American cheeseburger!

I also began to build my personal "board of advisors." **Having people you can reach out to when you're not certain you're making the right decision, or when you have a situation and you're uncertain about asking particular questions within your environment, really makes a difference.** These "sounding-board" relationships have given me more courage to take a stand for what I feel strongly about, even in moments when I doubt myself because I don't have that particular experience.

# Heroic Busyness

Leaders' lives are filled with many things that need to be done and decisions that need to be made. You can be so focused on being productive that you feel guilty if you have any downtime. **Busyness can sometimes appear to be a badge of honor.** Even when you don't need to be busy, you probably carry your phone with you and constantly check it out of habit.

One Saturday afternoon, three friends and I went to our favorite lunch spot. We always eat at the bar and always have the same bartender, Tom. All four of us sat in a row on the stools, and each one of us was staring into our phones and emails. Tom was standing in front of us, quietly waiting. After a few minutes, he said, "Really, guys, is there a reason you came together to eat?"

This is not an unusual setting; you see this all the time. But the inability to take downtime, to enjoy friends, or to talk about things that don't equate to checking off a box on your "to-do" list, is robbing you of your energy and long-term health. I used to fill every waking hour with required activity, but it was often filled with things I didn't necessarily like to do.

Laura Vanderkam, author of *I Know How She Does It*, is a master of productivity. She has studied what high-powered women do with their 168 hours each week. She offers that you are not short of time, but rather you need to choose how you are going to use it. That 168 hours will feel very different if you are using more of your hours to do the things you enjoy doing.[4]

How you recharge your batteries can be unique to you, but it is important that you understand what you need and that you *make time* **for recovery.**

---

## CONVICTION WITH MY CALENDAR

In the past, I felt guilty about blocking time in my calendar to think or recuperate. I am now not accessible at all times for meetings or business matters. I cannot work non-stop and be effective. My mood is affected, as well as my ability to perceive nuances, and most certainly my patience. In other words, **my effectiveness as a leader correlates directly with my ability to restore energy.** I control my calendar, including weekends, to have the much-needed breaks for personal time, thought, and restoration. Everyone's cadence is different, and there is not a prescription on what is best. I have found what works for me, and my daily schedule reflects it. I may still feel guilty, but I now have a feeling of conviction!

**Susan Huppertz**
VP Global Operations | TE Connectivity

# The Essential Recovery

Our Signature Program participants take the TIGNUM Sustainable High Performance Index. This simple survey is designed to quickly assess your current habits and their impact on your executional stamina, mental agility, and resilience. It might not be a huge surprise that for every class the collective scores are lowest in the recovery section. In fact, almost 50% score below a 2.7 out of 5 in this category; pretty low scores for normally high-achieving women!

## Recovery is always given the short shrift.

If recovery time is so important for our health, why do we not prioritize it? In "How to Make Time for Yourself," an article in the November 2015 issue of *MORE* magazine, Susan Gregory Thomas pulls from a variety of resources and studies on this difficult challenge. One reason people don't prioritize recovery, she says, could be FOMO, or "Fear of Missing Out." We will invest our time into things we feel we need to be part of, or so we can be seen. But taking recovery time is essential.[5]

There is now adequate research from neuroscience that supports downtime as a critical component of our ability to grow and understand ourselves better along the way. We will never evolve and become all we can be if we don't invest in ourselves each day. And if we forgo that investment in our growth and learning for the immediate emergencies at work, it will affect our long-term health and happiness.

**Being busy is such a habit that the very notion of "unplugging" and taking downtime has to be learned.**

My daughter challenged me to take just 30 minutes a day to do nothing. At first, I found that to be excruciatingly painful. I couldn't just sit there, so I started by picking up a magazine that didn't require any intellectual muscle and just flipped through it. My mind began to wander, and it was very calming. My daughter was right.

**Doing nothing IS actually doing ... and letting your mind daydream is restorative.**

# Eugenia Ulasewicz

## There wasn't a normal path when I started my career. And even if there was, I don't think any of us would say we took it.

I am wired to move forward, not back. I am wired to appreciate the past, not to think "I should have … ," "I could have … ," "I would have … ." My parents had a really positive influence on me. They were very encouraging and would say, "You know, you can do whatever you want to do." My dad was a corporate business executive, and my mother was a teacher. At the age of 60, she charted a new chapter and became an interior designer, becoming President of her local ASID chapter in her mid 60s. For some reason, I took a course in fashion marketing in college, and that professor changed my life. I did this 180 and never looked back.

## My 50s were about achieving. My 60s are about doing.

Starting so early in the day, finishing so late at night, and not getting enough sleep while juggling your responsibilities — career, being a mom and spouse — is very hard to do, but you do it when you're working your way up. By the time I was in my late 50s, I had been at it for a long time. As President of

*Eugenia is a Non-Executive Director of three public boards*

Burberry, Americas, I was the second oldest employee, worldwide, with 70% of the people who worked there under the age of 30.

Sixty was a magic number for me. I wanted my 60s to be about making a difference — about putting my thumbprint on something. And I wanted to live a healthy life. I needed to give myself time and space to focus on things that were pulling at me: a desire for more regular exercise, more spontaneity and fun, more time to learn new things, and more opportunities to use my abilities in new ways.

## My coach challenged me to do two things: meet other senior women outside of my regular network in the retail world, and stop and listen to my heart.

So I joined the Committee of 200 and Women's Forum New York. Both organizations consist of a group of very creative corporate and entrepreneurial women who have really successful careers. My C200 Council represents several decades of experience and huge breadth across industries. They are a significant support group for whatever I have to navigate. At first, putting myself out there at major gatherings of professional organizations made me feel like I was a duck out of water, but I didn't just show up. I went prepared and did my homework on who was there and where I wanted to spend my time. My only regret was not starting sooner to expand my network outside of my industry.

I'm very intentional and passionate about this next chapter. I have always been devoted to helping younger women achieve their potential through mentoring and participating as a Visiting Chair at New York University Gallatin School. A young woman I coached gave me a pillow with the word "Mentor" on it. It has a special place in my office, and reminds me daily how much joy I receive by spending time here.

I also love the business of business. Serving on three very different public boards keeps me engaged in a stimulating and challenging arena. Being a board member is very different than running a company, but I love it. It

gets me out of bed every day, keeps me learning, and allows me to contribute in a significant way.

## I can't draw a thing. But I am creative in my own way.

I spent a big part of my life thinking I wasn't creative. I remember my mother asking my art teacher in Grade 4 how she could give me a C in art. "You obviously don't understand her and how goal-orientated she is. If you give her a C, she's going to think she's terrible and become discouraged. She'll get turned off of art and never appreciate it. Is that really the message you want to give her, just because she can't draw?" That was the only C I ever got.

Today, sitting in a New York hotel lobby, I am waiting for the sale of our family home to close. Photos on my phone remind me of my home office, which is filled with light. It is a space I created to give myself time to explore who I am that is separate from being "president of X company."

## The value of having my own space for creating this next episode of my life is clear; everything in it helps me stay connected with joy, keeps me present, and helps me think about things differently.

Mentoring, helping other women to fulfill their dreams, my ongoing board work, and my golf game are four areas in which I am still learning, still growing, still raising the bar. I wonder what I will create next.

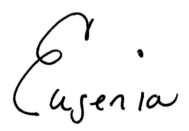

# The Three Rs

When I'm feeling overwhelmed and need to make an adjustment, I practice my Three Rs. **RELAX** is first. I'll take a walk, garden, get a massage — anything that takes me away from the office. Without this, you can continue to spiral.

While I'm relaxing, I **REFLECT** on where I am and where I want to go. If it's a work issue or challenge, I reflect on the job at hand. Where am I in that process? Who do I need support from to get the job done? Reflection is powerful because you take the time to remember and imagine the situation differently. Without reflection, you're really not learning anything you can leverage in the future.

The last R is **REGROUP**, which is when I reassess my plan and make adjustments. Regrouping is about prioritization and creating the go-forward plan.

## Canda Carr
**VP Global Channel Sales | TE Connectivity**

I love the way Canda Carr approaches how to create energy and keep moving forward. She incorporates a practice of Three Rs.

There is a long list of cognitive benefits to downtime. It increases your overall productivity and your ability to engage with people, think creatively, and solve problems.

## If Not Now, When?

You can plan to do many things, but plans are just plans if you never find the time to "get around to it." You can have many opportunities placed right in front of you, yet defer them to "a better time."

I have so often played this scenario over and over in my head; "Oh, I will go take that hike next weekend," or "As soon as I finish this project, I will go see a movie." Every time, the opportunity passes. There is no next time. Life becomes a string of non-stop deferrals. Sadly, those are simple examples. You can have a long list of much more meaningful "next times" when you defer spending quality time with a close friend, or even your child. When discussing the challenges of our busy lives over dinner, Leslie Pchola, Area VP Operations Southeast at Hilton Worldwide, simply stated:

**"You have 24 hours in a day and you get to choose what those should look like."**

## Dialing Down Energy-Robbing Activities

There are many factors in your life that rob you of your energy. Some of those are self-inflicted, like letting your mindset get off track and pull you into a spiral of self-limiting beliefs. Others, like jammed schedules and changing requests for your time, are a challenge to manage. Whenever we discuss the crazy schedules that all of our executives in the Signature Network keep, I often find myself thinking back to my blizzard Monday.

> "I was on far too many committees, and leaning in too much, thinking it was good for my career. Sometimes you need to lean out."

### Susan Beat
**Former Managing Director | MUFG Union Bank, N.A.**

---

## Blizzard Monday

One Sunday night, as I was preparing for my full day of meetings on Monday, Atlanta was hit with an ice storm. Atlanta lacks the equipment needed for these infrequent events and was rendered paralyzed, not just for a few hours, but for several days. On that Monday, all of the meetings I had set up were also "shut down." That day became a totally free day. Without a single meeting to interrupt my focus, it was a day that became very productive. All of my colleagues had the same pleasant windfall of productivity, so we decided to have a "blizzard day" once a month for the entire office — a day with no meetings or phone calls. These days also had huge benefits on relationship-building, as it gave us more time together in a non-structured way.

Managing the cadence of our days directly impacts our energy and productivity. Kim Bailes took a more thoughtful approach to her day and discovered a path back to quality thinking.

## When I Was Too Available

I have a natural tendency to have an open-door policy. I'm in an office amongst a large team, some of whom are my direct reports, but the others all come and carry out their business with me. I'm highly collaborative and like to ensure that I'm also real-time coaching our younger team members, but I recognized that **having an open-door policy was not always helping me focus on other priorities** that I needed to be thinking about for my broader business. It wasn't allowing me to take that step back, to think on a more strategic level and where I might want to reposition certain aspects.

So I tried shutting my door for short periods and then reopening it. I sought feedback for the change I made and, surprisingly to me, people said "Well, I think it's quite natural in your leadership role that you would have to have some time where you would require privacy and focus." This positive result showed me that **you can move around the way you have always behaved and gain from the rebalancing**.

### Kim Bailes
**Global Head of Loan Sales, Syndicated Finance | ING Bank N.V.**

# Heather Milligan

## *Always step outside of yourself and reach backward to help the people behind you.*

My passion is around the successes of people; supporting them, accessing resources for them, getting them engaged with the right ideas, and watching them grow. Happiness follows that passion — and so do revenues and earnings.

I'm very aware of the people who have taken time out of their busy lives to reach back and help me — so many people I can't even count them all. I came into the business world from a very different path than most executives at my level.

At 16, I graduated from high school. I moved out with, literally, nothing. I had to find a way to sustain myself. My first job as a records clerk made me $10,500 a year. I thought I had won the lottery! I didn't even have the wardrobe to play the part. Other people loaned me professional-looking skirts and blouses to wear.

Humility, a desire to please people, and a fear of failure were my companions right out of the gate, as was my insatiable curiosity about the world. I wanted to talk with every person, learn every job. My company was a great support in this. They paid for me to go to night school at a technical college and then invested in me to go on to university. I didn't let those opportunities go to waste. I've held 19 different positions in the 26 years I've been with this company.

*Heather is the SVP Underwriting & New Business of Lincoln Financial Group*

I've been through three M&As, career advances, lateral moves, and even one backward move.

In 1999, three major life events hit all in one month; I miscarried; I discovered that my 3-year-old son has Asperger's, a form of autism that can be a debilitating learning disability; and I read in the paper that my real father had died and that I had four siblings whom I had never met. My boss, who had earmarked me to succeed him, gave me his empowering support and made it possible for me to stay with the company through these trials. He arranged it so I could step out of a leadership role and take on an individual contributor role.

**My focus shifted from success and getting better to balance and being authentic.** At work, I started to do some travel and to really build more of a broad business base. Success came quite quickly. Now I run a risk management shop, underwriting new business for life insurance. I wouldn't change anything in my life, especially not the challenges that were my greatest learning opportunities.

Integrity is the most prized possession. For me, leading with integrity is about finding that balance between empowering people and delegating responsibility. I work really hard at making sure we get every drop of wisdom from everyone at the corporate leadership table. The same goes with my team. I give everyone permission to have a voice. At the same time, I hold people accountable. I'm there to give them support and resources, but to maintain that balance, too. Very rarely do I need to pull out the "boss" card.

**I work a lot, but I never let that interfere with my core of support: my husband and my son.**

My son is my inspiration. As a child, he had to learn how to read people's emotions and be sensitive to them. He had a full-time aide with him in the classroom all the way through grade school. But when he went to high school, he told us he wanted to do it on his own — without an aide. When he chose to leave high school at 16 to go to college three hours away, we supported him in that choice as well. Now my son, someone who is hypersensitive to touch and sound and incredibly gifted when it comes to language, is a senior at university. Whenever I feel like things are overwhelming, I think about what he has done and the kind of focus and determination it has taken for him to be true to himself and successful in his own way. Looking at him, I know that if he can do anything, I can, too.

*Heather*

# Unloading Your Packages

One of the best mentors I ever had gave me this tip. Every night when you leave work, you probably walk by the same trees, find your car in the same parking spot, pass by the same buildings on your way home. Every night, package up all the things that are weighing on your mind that seem so important. Imagine yourself putting those packages in specific places along the way on your journey home: in that tree, in that mailbox, in that building. When you come back in the morning, make a conscious decision which packages you will pick up to bring with you back to work. You will find that the packages will always be lighter in the morning than when you left them there the night before. The same works for packages from home.

**Things are never as big and onerous or as bad and overwhelming as they were the night before when you walked out the door with them.**

*Every woman who's trying to juggle it all really needs to stay true to herself on at least a few things. If you need to go to yoga class, or take a run, do it, because that personal element of what's going to keep you centered and strong is so critical to maintaining your family leadership and your work leadership.*

Devry Boughner Vorwerk
Corporate VP, Global Corporate Affairs | Cargill

# Setting Boundaries

Deciding how to use your 24 hours each day may seem straightforward, but many executives find that the most difficult part of that decision comes when they have to set boundaries. Remember, Wikipedia says, "How you treat yourself is how you are inviting the world to treat you." If you make yourself available 24 hours a day, seven days a week, others will begin to expect that from you. Elsa Amouzgar, VP – General Manager, Global Sales at ManpowerGroup, shares how her view of setting boundaries has changed over the years. She has moved beyond feelings of guilt and makes a point to include non-company activities in her regular routine (see her story on page 40).

Not only does your hectic schedule impact you, but so do the people you connect with.

When surrounded by energy, you get energy. There are times when you need a "pick-me-up." I have a few people that, when I just hear their voice, I feel lighter and more positive because they exude that upbeat energy. But there are also people that can suck energy from you. They are the people that, when you see their name appear on your cell phone, you cringe and send it to voicemail.

**Choosing whom we spend our time with is just as important as choosing what goes on our calendar. It's all about choices.**

## Saying No

This seems to be one of the hardest things for women to do. Hundreds who have taken part in the "Gift Exercise" from Chapter One (see page 11) recorded their highest energy moments and lowest energy moments over 30 days. Activities that showed up in the Energy Depleters column were often ones they had a choice to say no to!

Sometimes you get pulled into last-minute emergency meetings that are important, but can make you feel out of control. When your calendar gets hijacked, it takes some intentionality to examine whether you have choices, or different options, to meet the request. Teresa Purtill describes what happened to her and how she changed her normal tendency to put herself last (see page 115).

**When under stress, this may be the very best time to spend on "self-care." Choosing to spend time with people who give you energy, or where you can provide your gifts to others, is a great way to practice self-care.**

Teresa was also able to give a member of her team a great development opportunity in presenting to the CFO, which showed that she had confidence in her.

Spend time on the things where you can use your gifts to have the greatest impact.

## Intersection of Important and Urgent

Not everything can be as important and as urgent as everything else, because then you're just busy.

I like delivering on my promises, but I realize you also cannot say yes to everything, all the time. That actually means that everything that you're trying to do is equally important. The reality is, it isn't. What I see happening in the workplace and when I talk to peers is that we neglect to think about what's important *and* what's urgent.

Busy is okay, but busy isn't going to make you do something profoundly different, or creative, or groundbreaking.

**Annemieke van der Werff**
**Chief Human Resources Officer for the Americas | MUFG Union Bank**

# Deborah Jackson

## What I do every day has an impact beyond me.

No woman has ascended to the CEO level of a major investment bank.

At a certain point, I just did not see a path, an open door to move upward. I knew I could play out years of doing more of the same thing. It would have been lucrative, but I wanted more. I was getting very restless and hungry to learn more, to do more. I knew it was time.

When I decided to leave Wall Street, I gave myself several years to experiment and find the way I could make the biggest contribution.

**The only thing I really felt excited about was visionary female entrepreneurs I met who were founding companies with something new in mind. They were really passionate about what they were doing to make the world better.**

I thought, "I want to be over there with companies that are building the future." That's why I started Plum Alley, an investment platform to help female entrepreneurs raise capital. Now I work with visionaries and innovators who are founding companies and creating new products and services. The founders may be broke, or working like crazy, but they are motivated, passionate, and alive with excitement for what they are building. I was drawn to that. It is important to me to know that the companies that we fund would probably have died on the vine if we hadn't funded them. To me, there's nothing more satisfying than knowing we've given them that lifeline for a while.

*Deborah*

## Never Underestimate the Power of Women

Climbing the ladder in corporate America is so often about how you fit into the culture and make a contribution. You need to offer solutions to problems. And you need other people who support and advance you. You don't do that by being the contrarian all the time. You do that by building a consensus of the group.

When I started on Wall Street in 1980, there was only a handful of women in executive positions. We weren't in the mainstream. It was very difficult to move up into the highest levels of running the firm. That is still true today.

*Deborah is the Founder and CEO of Plum Alley*

# Downward Spiral

It's so easy to revert to usual patterns of behavior when in a stressful situation. I was scheduled to be at The Signature Program for a panel, and I got a last-minute notice calling me to a budget finalization meeting on the same dates. It, actually, was to present my year-forward budget to the CFO. Typically, everything that's good for me goes out the window when I am panicked. What you really need to do though, in these situations, is invest in yourself and stick to what you know you need to do to be successful in the tough times. **If I look back on my career, it's when I needed this attention the most that I let things spiral downward.** These are the very things that fuel a positive mindset and positive body. When this conflict came up, I was ready to cancel and go do the work. Instead, I thought to myself,

## I'm not going to ask, I'm going to tell.

I said to my boss, "I appreciate that next week is going to be very busy, so I have briefed Nicola, and obviously, it's important that she attend in my absence."

"Where are you going to be?" he asked.

I thought to myself, "There is nothing, physically, that I can do to get us more ready for the presentation, and I've got a team of people who can work on it in my absence." So I said, "I'm committed in Brussels for a panel, but Nicola will represent us well." I went home to my husband and said, "I am insane, going to Brussels given what I have going on this week, but that's exactly why I need to go."

Teresa Purtill

Head of Customer Operations | Bord Gáis Energy

# Linda Knoll

*If it's not right for your personal life right now, it will never be right for your professional life.*

At age 37, I had my first offer to be a General Manager. It was the dream job. It was truly beyond my wildest expectations. Up to this point, I had taken many risks and lateral moves to do a lot of different roles to, hopefully, prepare myself for an opportunity like this.

But when the opportunity arrived, I had just gotten divorced and had two young kids. The role required a move. It was absolutely the wrong time in my personal life. I kept telling myself from a professional point of view, "I can't come up with any reason to say no." But from a personal point of view, I had all kinds of reasons.

I concluded that if it wasn't going to be right for me, how could it possibly be right for the company? So I turned it down. The company was fantastic about it and agreed that if it isn't really the time now, the time will come, and it did. Two years later, the company was completely changing. It was undergoing a merger. All new management came in and I was offered a different general manager role. When I look back at it now, okay, it happened at 39 instead of 37, but I know we made the right call. It's still the best job I ever had.

*Linda is the Chief Human Resources Officer of CNH Industrial, N.V. and Chief Human Resources Officer of Fiat Chrysler Automobiles, N.V.*

## You've got to give people space. If you do, they will occupy it.

It's hard sometimes to let go of managing what is happening on a day-to-day basis, but you create a sense of empowerment by leaning on others to manage what you may have managed before. You've got to give people the reins and really let go. You are not going to create capacity by yourself. You do it with others.

## On Paper, It was Perfect

### You can't have your eyes so focused on what is directly in front of your face that you miss the view on the horizon.

Early in my career, running multiple manufacturing plants, we faced a significant industry downturn. We were constantly reviewing how to change our industrial footprint so that we could take down fixed costs. We came up with a proposal that, as ugly as it was, called for closing a plant and transferring product to another facility within our footprint.

The financial analysis said it was the right thing to do. The payback was outstanding. The technical fit for the receiving plant was sound. The commercial guys were happy. The plan, on paper, was perfect.

The executive committee confirmed the proposal made sound business sense, so we went forward. We announced the plan publicly. We advised employees that the plant would be closing in 12 months. We started to ready ourselves. We met with our dealer principals and all of those kind of things you need to do. Guess what happened? The industry changed, and it changed very quickly. We actually had to go back and **reverse everything**.

When somebody asks me, "What's the biggest mistake you've made?," it's this. This one eats at me because, as the head of manufacturing, I owned the plan. I learned the hard way that if the input you start with is flawed, the rest of your plan is flawed. Our industry projection was so very wrong. Thank God we were able to course correct.

The employees of that plant were incredibly understanding and appreciative that we were humble enough to go back and say, "We made a mistake." Despite causing that kind of incredibly ugly impact on their lives, the employees appreciated the honesty that management is not perfect.

## Leadership is a Privilege

Our CEO, Sergio Marchionne, says,

### "Leadership is a privilege. It's a privilege that you earn every day. It's about having a sense of duty, appreciating that leadership is a sacred trust, something you can never abuse. If you don't respect this privilege, you will lose it."

# Ellie Patsalos

**I'm not going to change for anyone. If you don't like me, fine. I will go somewhere else where they want me.**

I grew up in a small village in Cyprus. The traditional expectation as a daughter in a family of seven children was for me to finish school, get married, and have a child by the time I was 18, like my sisters had done.

My dad was very forward-looking and felt that English was the language of the future. He insisted I go to the American academy instead of the Greek school I wanted to go to. In the summer of 1972, family from the UK visited us, and that enabled me to push, and pray, and ask my father's blessing to leave school and go to England to study. In some ways, this was a bit of a revolt from my family. I had to promise to return and marry after graduation. After one year at A level, I was offered a spot at the London School of Economics. With a husband in waiting, I convinced my father to allow me to go do my MBA for one year before returning. **That was a white lie**; I never went back.

I met my husband in London. He wanted to go to America and do his post-doctorate training, and I said, "Yeah, America! Wow!" That was enticing. We married

and moved to Texas because cowboys and hot weather sounded interesting. I got a job in tax support for a large Texas company and we began our family. With our extended family in the UK, we decided to return. We agreed that my job would become the growth focus, and my career took off soon after. As a junior person at Deloitte, I was placed on the Bloomberg account, and I ran with it. I found I had a true gift for developing and growing global clients. I was even nicknamed, "Ms. Bloomberg," as it grew to be the largest and longest-running client in my portfolio.

I speak fast and use my hands a lot. I always dress fashionably, in miniskirts and bright colors, but **the firm wanted me to tone down my style to be more like the other women partners.** I wasn't going to change for anyone. Take it or leave it. I became partner and finished my career at Deloitte at the mandatory retirement age of 60.

I didn't intend to be on the board, but I was asked to step up and take an important female leadership role. I was elected to the maximum allowed of three terms. My legacy is about developing young people so they can own the work. Then I let go. Now, I have carved out another chapter that includes client work, several charities, staying healthy and active, mentoring young women, and time for travel and family. I'm headed to climb Mt. Kilimanjaro to support one of my charities, Breast Cancer Now.

*Ellie*

---

*Ellie is the Managing Director and Founder of Patsalos Consulting Ltd.*

## Sleep Your Way to Skinny

One way to use some of your 24 hours in a day is to recover through sleep. Lack of enough sleep is another major source of energy depletion for executives who often live with jam-packed, travel-filled, and extremely irregular schedules.

Recent research equates lack of sleep to weight gain. When I heard that on the radio, I wondered if I could sleep my way to skinny. Maybe it's not quite that simple, but lack of sleep does have a significantly negative impact on many areas of your life. Your ability to cope with stressful situations, to really listen to your colleagues and team, or to create and stick to a high-performance plan for nutrition can all be diminished due to lack of sleep. At lunch one day, Pam Kimmet, CHRO at Cardinal Health, and I compared our heavy international travel schedules and ideas for how to get rest. She quipped,

### "Sleep is the best accessory."

Ann Fandozzi also knows the importance of sleep. When I asked Ann what was the one thing she could not do without when she traveled, her answer made me laugh out loud.

### "I cannot do without my own pillow. It's a full-size, goose-down pillow, and I only ever take a carry-on bag. It's because *sleep is so essential*. Going from hotel room to hotel room is a little bit disorienting, but when your head hits your pillow, it knows it's time to go to sleep."

## Say Yes to the Right Things and No to Everything Else

*We have a hard time saying no. Oftentimes, I try to think about it as saying yes to the right things. It's a journey. You want to please your boss, you want to do the right thing, you want to solve the problem, you want to be all things, to all people, in all aspects of your life, but the reality is, you can't. It is about a choice in that moment.*

### Sometimes saying no is the most powerful thing you can do.

*I used to think when I was talking to my boss, "He really knows what I want." Now I realize, if I'm not saying what I want, I am not being very clear. Sometimes you get caught up with, am I doing what I want to do? Am I doing the things that I find energy with? I happen to be good at the stuff that I don't find energy-inducing. I'm not bringing in the energy every day because I happen to just say yes to the things that maybe aren't important to me. For me, linking the times to say no and the times to say yes shows what you need, where you want to spend your time, and what's important to you.*

**Kathleen Valentine**
General Manager, Prescription Drug Monitoring and Toxicology
| Quest Diagnostics, Inc.

# Lisa Butler

I find that when we look at other successful women, we so often assume, "Hey, they're smart. It must have been easy to get to where they are." Yet everyone has something traumatic that they've gone through, either earlier in their life or in midlife, that they have used as a catalyst to get where they are today.

**There's so much more underneath, so much more that we can learn from each other, if we would only just ask ... and share.**

Women need to understand that everyone's had a crisis. It's not until we go through it, come out the other side, and

*Lisa is the VP of Strategy of MotionPoint*

## *I had decided I could never tell anyone about what I had overcome because they would judge me differently.*

talk about it that we begin to create a framework in which everyone can come together and talk about how to get through adversity.

When I was still in college, I was hit by a drunk driver who was attempting to commit suicide. After being flown by helicopter to an ER, I was in the hospital for over a month with a head injury, then in rehab. I'm lucky to be walking. I'm lucky to be speaking and writing. And I'm lucky that the best plastic surgeon was on call that night.

Before then, I wasn't sure what my path was going to be. I wasn't taking college seriously. I wasn't focused and driven. I just didn't know what I wanted to do or what I wanted to be. The accident had me reassess what was important — focus and career — and remember that it is up to me to make the right decisions and do the right things to get to where I'm safe. After all, no one is going to take care of me but me. That accident made me who I am today.

Nothing seems as hard as what I went through recovering from that. So now, whenever I'm faced with tough challenges, I go back to these thoughts:

**I'm not dying. No one else is dying. This isn't brain surgery. We're going to get through this.**

# I Can't Sleep

Heard often, but its cause can be rooted in many sources. First, do a diagnostic.

Do you have a consistent routine when you go to bed? This might sound crazy if you are traveling the globe and changing time zones, but we don't think it's crazy when we establish a routine for our child or our pet. Creating a nighttime ritual that signals wind-down and relaxation before hitting the bed is insurance for a restful night. When you align with a ritual, it neurologically adjusts hormones.

Are you consistent when you go to bed? Do you unwind with a breathing routine? Maybe a favorite pillow or noise machine can signal "it's time." Ninety minutes before bedtime, start to move away from laptops, cellphones, and other blue-light sources, which are known for blocking our melatonin production, our natural preparation for sleep.

Here are some additional tips for creating those ZZZs.

ZZZ Watch your exercise too close to bedtime, as it increases neurotransmitters and hormones not conducive to sleep

ZZZ Don't charge your cell phone right next to your bed. Research shows EMF radiation (also from laptops, microwaves, and even light outlets) in close proximity may keep you from sleeping

ZZZ Incorporate essential oils, like lavender on your pillow, or ingest natural botanicals like Kava, lemon balm, or chamomile tea to induce sleep

ZZZ Wind down your mind with a focus and reflection on three to five things that went really well during the day. If that ruminating starts, try a deep breathing technique or meditation

ZZZ Create the environment. Low lights, candles, nice smells, calming music, low voices, and favorite sheets. Pack items in your suitcase that are part of creating your sleep routine

# Play and Creativity

Setting boundaries allows you to dial into all the aspects of self-care, including taking time to let go and enjoy the freedom of having fun. You know how good you feel when you laugh, or play games, or just let your mind wander. And there is now scientific knowledge on how play and creativity can provide health and performance benefits. But you have to be willing to give yourself permission to spend time on these things. Each day, when I drive into the parking lot of the community center to swim, I see the sign at the entrance:

## Play at your own risk

I chuckle. Does that mean I risk liking it and then finally understand what I have been missing?

There is a National Institute for Play. Yes, that's right. Founder Dr. Stuart Brown, a well-known psychologist, has gathered a wide body of thinkers, doctors, and researchers and now has clinical evidence that links play deprivation during the formative years to people becoming serial killers. The Institute makes the case that play and creativity are vital to our health, and just as pervasive as sleep.[6]

### "The opposite of play is not work. The opposite of play is depression."

I remember a meeting with our CEO, early in my career. I sat down in the chair across from his desk. The office was a typical CEO office — a blotter, books, all dark wood, an expensive pen, and a few photos in heavy frames. As we were talking, I looked over and saw a new box of crayons on his desk. "What's that, Carter?" He reached over and handed me the box and said, "Open it. Now close your eyes and smell it." It took me back to my grade-school days, when I was always so excited to buy new school supplies and to anticipate the start of a new school year. It's good to have a trigger like that to make you remember and reflect on simple things, fun things, and important things.

## Your Environment, Your Attitude

Your environment has a lot to do with your energy, too. I recently revamped my whole office to incorporate things that give me energy. Natural light is key, but since I work into the evening, the lighting for after-hours has to be warm and inviting. I have both a stand-up and sitting desk, and my space is filled with colors that I love. Eugenia Ulasewicz, former President Americas for Burberry and a Non Executive Director of several other public companies (see her story on page 106), talks about how her new space is helping her creativity. She also uses her travel time to embrace those environments, which stimulate her creative processes.

"I always take a pair of sneakers with me. No matter where I am in the world,

### "I can take those 10,000 steps every day. I can explore where I am, keeping my head up as I'm observing things, even if it's just the daffodils in London in early February, the ocean boardwalk in Barcelona, or the Washington DC mall in September."

# Peace Produces Results

I now believe that the way we work can make a difference in our performance. There are a thousand choices, every day, that can either add to, or rob us of, our energy. I have been a world champion at cruising from one meeting to another, and I realized how powerful scheduled breaks are. I'm now using 15 to 20 minutes, mid-day, for a quick walk away from the office to get out of the environment. I am also moving locations to sit elsewhere in the building, and it improves my ability to concentrate on new things. I realize that all conversations are important, and I am now setting outcomes for them and being clear on what I want out of them. I have been using the power of reframing and asking myself, "What is my mindset, and how can I give the conversation energy?"

**Hanne Søndergaard**
**EVP and Chief Marketing Officer | Arla Foods amba**

The right environment can also help you feel comfortable. Pat Wadors, the CHRO of LinkedIn, published a blog on being an introvert in Silicon Valley and relayed how much energy it took to demonstrate extrovert behaviors. To help her, she created an office space that felt as comfortable as a living room. That comfortable setting helped her engage people in conversations. She also learned that the power of body language can show engagement without her needing to speak a word.[7]

Just moving into a new environment can change your entire perspective. Getting up from your chair, taking a walk, using a different route to the cafeteria, even taking a power nap in the car during your lunch hour are all great ways to reset and rejuvenate. Try using "walking meetings" as a way to get fresh air while having a conversation with your employee to review a plan, or tackle an issue. It accomplishes two goals at the same time; the ability to get into a different environment allows the mind to power up.

In a recent call with some of our Wisdom Warriors, we reviewed coping mechanisms for dealing with stress. This comment stuck out.

## "Changing your physiology changes your psychology."

All of these tools — setting boundaries, finding the right environment, play, recovery, and sleep — can help you sustain your energy and bring your best self to work, and to life. But we still only have 24 hours in a day and 365 days in a year. As we discovered in Chapter Two, we have to manage our capacity at a macro level to allow these tools to do their jobs.

# Sarena Lin

## *I think with leadership there is no such thing as a set path to an A. It has to fit your personal values and style.*

*Sarena is the President, Cargill Feed & Nutrition of Cargill*

I grew up in a very traditional Chinese environment with family values of working hard, respecting the culture of authority and seniority, and having "grit." As long as you do your best, you will get there. My dad grew up in a very poor, rural area of Taiwan, as one of eight children. He was the only one from his family who went to college. My mom was one of 11, and also the only one from her family to go to college. Both my parents were professors.

I studied computer science when I was an undergrad, then went to business school. When I joined McKinsey & Company after I graduated, the definition of success suddenly changed.

**Being a student, in some ways, was easy. You know what it takes to get an A, but no one can define for you what an A looks like at work.**

When I first went to Harvard, I felt a little uncomfortable. When I went to McKinsey, I felt very uncomfortable. I stepped into the room and thought, "All of these smart people are around me, and I don't think as fast or speak English very well."

After my very first project review, my manager pulled me aside and said, "Sarena, I noticed that you didn't say anything in the meeting." I said, "But you have all my work." He said, "That's not good enough." It was the very first time in my life that I was told that I was not good enough. I was so used to following directions of what I needed to do and working through it myself.

**I suddenly realized my roadmap had completely changed. In fact, it's not even charted.**

I learned the following year that if you don't speak at the meetings, people don't really recognize what you do. If you don't contribute to the debates, people don't understand your thinking capability. If you don't stand up for what you believe in, people will think you are a doer, but not really committed.

I thought I would stay with McKinsey for two years, and I ended up being there 13 years. When I was elected partner, I was given the reins to lead the McKinsey office in Taiwan. I doubled the size of the office in two years. Building a team of high-performing consultants to tackle the most challenging business problems in a fast-growing economy was a fantastic experience.

When I joined Cargill to lead what is now Corporate Strategy & Development, I had a team of 90. They were a smart, rather homogeneous group. Two years ago, I was asked to lead Cargill Animal Feed and Nutrition. All of a sudden, I went from a team of 90 in four locations to 15,000 in more than 200 locations around the world. People don't care how smart I am, or my ability to drive "strategy," because we have a function for that.

I had self-doubts and thought, "Why do I deserve to be a leader of this group? What do I bring to the table?"

My preconceived notion was to prove myself. Therefore, I better show what I know. I quickly learned the past was not going to get me to where I needed to go.

**I had to let go of my traditional "grit" and get out of my comfort zone. I had to figure out what it was going to take to help my team and my business be successful in the next phase.**

As I was reminded, I am here to lead and empower the team so they can go all out and do the best in their respective roles.

I couldn't have asked for a better assignment and challenge. I have been chosen to add value, and I believe I am in the right role. I needed to give myself time to learn the business and how we make money. I spent a lot of time asking questions and asking my team to help me learn. I realized that the more I listened, the more I saw how talented the team was, and how much more they can take on. With more trust and credibility two years into this, I'm giving myself a bit more permission to lead from the front.

At Cargill, we started a transformation journey about two years ago. I continue to ask the questions of how my team can add value to help our on-the-ground employees be truly successful. What do we need to change? How do we need to show up? How do we behave? I think those are some of the fun things that I'm dealing with, and it is what gets me energized and excited every day.

Adjusting your leadership style as you go is a never-ending journey. Understanding the team composition, understanding the organizational energy, and knowing how you fit in, at this point in time, allows you to make the proper adjustments. It's about learning which adjustments work and trying to figure it out as you go.

*Sarena*

# Making Space — Repack Your Bag

Going 70 miles an hour, from morning to night, means that you have not allowed for any space in your life. Without space, you can't recognize an opportunity when it comes knocking, let alone act on it. And without space, the serendipitous fun just can't happen!

Years ago, I read the book *Repacking Your Bags: Lighten Your Load for the Good Life* by Richard Leider and David Shapiro. The authors make you take a hard look at all of those past patterns that can weigh you down. Consider how when you go on a trip, you pack a bag for that journey. When you come home, you unpack until the next trip. The problem with life is that you carry one bag and you forget to unpack anything. You just keep adding more into it until it becomes too heavy to carry around. What's inside that you don't need? Are there possessions, responsibilities, or even relationships that you are lugging along that you no longer should be?[8]

## To achieve sustained high energy, build in time for recovery

Signature grads who have intentionally built in recovery time have seen an average increase of 15% in sustained energy level throughout the workday and at home.

**TYPICAL DAY**
- Check emails before shower
- Energy bar/triple-shot coffee in the car
- Back-to-back meetings all day
- Lunch on the run
- Daughter's soccer game
- Eat "take-out" in the car
- Emails last hour before bed

**DAY WITH INTENTIONAL RECOVERY**
- Check news while eating nutritional breakfast
- Schedule 45-minute meetings with 15-minute breaks to plan
- Water bottle in hand all day
- 30-minute walking meeting with employee
- Breathing technique before big meeting
- Dinner with family — no phone
- Nighttime wind-down technique before bed

*SOURCE: Survey of 60 Executives from The Signature Program*

> "Everyone has a vision of what a perfect job and a perfect marriage looks like, of how their life is supposed to be and going to be. Best to put that on the shelf as an aspiration. You have to figure out what works for you at this point in time, and how you're going to organize your time from here."

**Leslie Pchola**
Area VP Operations S.E. | Hilton Worldwide

I think repacking your bag is a critical life skill, so each September, when it is typically back-to-school time for kids, I spend time thinking about my bag and what should be in it. I pick this time of year because back-to-school time is usually when you get to "start fresh" with a new teacher, new books, new classroom, and new supplies. It's almost as if you get to reinvent yourself and wipe the slate clean from the previous year.

The best way to do this "repacking" is to take everything out. Put the most important things back inside first. Then decide what can go in after that. But leave SPACE. **Without space, you cannot see opportunities that present themselves, let alone have any time to act on them.** Having space in your bag allows you to pick up interesting and unexpected items along the way.

# The Best You Is Best for Others, Too

Leadership is not about having a title. You have to bring your own signature style of leadership that is unique to you, and allows you to differentiate yourself and bring a better "you" to your organization, your team, your friends, and your family. Leticia Goncalves, President, Europe and Middle East for Monsanto, shared her perspective with a recent gathering of executive women leaders.

"We should always look to maximize our potential, not only by developing ourselves, but by understanding how it makes a difference when we can apply these teachings in our jobs. I came to the realization that if I can bring my A-game in everything I do, that's my best chance to win. And by being a better me, I am a better coach and leader for my team and my company."

Practicing self-care, intentionally building in recovery time throughout your day, ensuring you are getting the sleep and nutrition to maximize energy, and making time for play, fun, and laughter are all critical components to bringing out the best of you. And when the best of you shows up, it impacts everything you see and do.

# Katie Carter

> *It's always been women who have either stood next to me, or stood behind me, who have pushed me forward.*

It was a big decision. It was a lateral move. It was an easy decision, in the sense that I definitely wanted to move overseas. That was something that I'd wanted to do for a long time. That wasn't the difficult part. From a career perspective, was it the right decision?

I spent some time talking to people while at The Signature Program about their experiences with lateral moves and with moves to Asia. By the time I was done asking questions, I was really excited about the opportunity in Hong Kong. It has been a great experience for my family. It has been wonderful to watch my kids really flourish. My son went to an immersion program in Hangzhou, China, and called me, one of his first nights there. He was a bit homesick and asked, "Why did you send me to this boring program?" I'm thinking to myself, "All right. Just

*Katie is the VP Human Resources of Hyatt International Asia Pacific*

calm down, Katie, because he's going to thank you, one of these days." Professionally, the move has given me a new perspective of our business in Asia, a deeper dive.

My Dutch parents have been the biggest influences that shaped who I am today. My mother had a very clear focus on what she wanted to achieve. For the time, she was very much a feminist, supporting women's rights, active in sports. She was a golf and squash champion in Liberia at that time. She was a model. She sewed her own clothes. She was a chef and an entrepreneur. My father was an artist. He played the drums. He was an entertainer, a dreamer. People loved to be around him. He would make them laugh. Together, it was a really wonderful partnership that they had. I think I took a little bit of each of them.

Growing up in Monrovia, Liberia, I saw a lot of poverty, but also a lot of joy and happiness. Everything that I've ever wanted to do is about making a difference in this world for the human condition, and for how we engage with each other.

It's always been women who have either stood next to me, or stood behind me, who have pushed me forward. These women have really made a difference for me. They've believed in me, and they've pushed me beyond what I believe to be my capability.

Now I focus on how I can help make a difference for the people that I work with every single day.

*Katie*

# Advice to My Younger Self

It really is true what they say; you actually do start to enjoy life much more in your 40s and 50s. I think it's partly because you don't take yourself so seriously and partly because you no longer need to figure things out. Your whole metabolism changes — your weight, your face, your skin, your fertility, even how you think about money, family, and relationships. You start to get that "chill factor." After all, you have arrived and survived. Now it's about savoring every moment, enjoying the journey, and giving more.

**Abbe Luersman**
**Chief Human Resources Officer | Ahold Delhaize**

"The better part of one's life consists of his friendships."

— Abraham Lincoln

# Relationships

*I was responsible for more than half of our overall revenue growth. I was operating as I had always operated — working long hours and driving results. The time had come for the Board to name a new CEO. I felt my work showed I was ready for the job, but I knew in my gut that I lacked relationships with key decision-makers. One of my advisors said to me, "Carol, if you want to be CEO, then act like a CEO!" Great advice, but a little too late.*

They selected another executive from our team; someone who not only delivered results within our company, but who also spent time communicating our results and our challenges to the Board. He had taken the time to build key relationships in order to develop trust, gain advocates, and set himself up with the support structure he would need to succeed as a CEO.

The Board had made a good choice, for good reasons. Performance is important in the C-suite, but as a leader you need to be able to demonstrate more than operational competency. You must have the ability to connect, within the organization and outside the organization. In Chapter One, those connector skills were identified as what sets hallmark leadership apart. So it's wise to be intentional about building the network that you need, in order to be successful as a leader.

Throughout the stories in this book, leadership and life are two parts of the same whole. Relationships are no different. Many women in this book have mentioned their life partner as an instrumental influence in being where they are today. Strong, enduring, loving relationships give you energy, and fuel your confidence and your long-term health.

## Relationships are fundamental, and at the root of our well-being as humans. In business, they are at the root of our success.

Marcia Avedon, Senior VP of Human Resources, Communications, and Corporate Affairs at Ingersoll Rand, says,

"Everyone needs at least one confidante: a person who cares about you entirely and unconditionally supports you; who is there for you, even in the dark periods; and who has your best interests at heart. It might be a parent, a husband, or a friend. Whoever it is, this is the person you can really talk to about what's going on with a full and open heart, when you're in a rough spot, either personally or professionally. This is the person who, when things are out of balance and you feel like you can't go on, just cares so deeply about you that they will be really honest with you. This is the person you can confide in, knowing they will not be judgmental; the person you can count on to really try to help you get to a better place."

*Vulnerability takes practice, but it breeds trust. Being open with others and showing our authentic selves allows us to move our relationships in a positive direction.*

## Good Relationships Keep You Happier and Healthier

The link between good relationships and health and happiness was documented by Harvard researchers in the "Study of Adult Development." They tracked "two groups of men over the last 75 years to identify the psychosocial predictors of healthy aging." Their work pointed to three key findings:

- ❋ Loneliness is toxic. People who are more connected to others are happier, healthier, and live longer than those who are less well-connected;
- ❋ Quality counts. People who are surrounded with good, satisfying relationships in mid-life are the healthiest in later life; and
- ❋ Good relationships protect our bodies and our brains. People who are in relationships where they feel that they can count on each other when the going gets tough experience less memory decline later in life, compared to those who aren't.[1]

Those personal relationships provide a foundation that also helps you bring your best self to work. But in business, it requires more than one dedicated individual to enable your success. You need to build a set of connected, supportive relationships around you — relationships that support the family unit, relationships that advocate for you inside the organization, and relationships outside your organization — with people who can help keep your ideas fresh and relevant, but can also give you the "straight talk" you need to hear when working through tough situations.

When you enter the leadership ranks, you are now being paid for more than your functional expertise and your ability to manage business. You are also being paid for your judgment and your ability to create and motivate high-performing teams.

To get things done, you must be able to connect with your peers, colleagues, team members, direct reports, and employees in such a way that they see and relate to you as an executive *leader*, not a manager. Preparing to enter a senior-level role is about building the relational skills needed to stay at the top of your game.

The stories in this chapter should leave you with no doubt that this is not a distraction *from* your job. It is what will make you even more valuable *at* your job. We will explore the types of relationships you need to build to be successful and what it takes to build those.

# Canda Carr

*I put my willpower (stubbornness, as my mother called it) together with patience to tackle challenges.*

helped me finally get my college degree by continuing my education at several colleges over 15 years. Perseverance continues to be a significant factor in my leadership brand.

As I progressed in my career, I had to make a conscientious move from being a manager to a leader. Managers make sure employees come to work and contribute, and they manage people to achieve goals. Leadership is about inspiring and coaching people to be the best they can be and, as a result, making the company even better.

One of my core values is helping and developing people, so I really enjoy looking for the "gems" in the organization that might otherwise be overlooked or lost in the shuffle. I get a lot of satisfaction coaching these individuals to reach their full potential.

I certainly can't do it all, so building a high-performing team is key to creating capacity. I want my team to excel, grow, and move to even bigger roles, which makes building the bench throughout the organization extremely critical. My goal is to create a very diverse team that draws from different experiences, different cultures, and adjacent industries. When you get a high-performing, diverse team focused on a shared vision and goal, the rest is fairly easy.

I've been working full time since I was 18 years old. My parents were divorcing when I finished high school, so my college education wasn't a priority. I really wanted to be a flight attendant, but after interviewing, I realized it wasn't for me. I ended up getting a job as a manufacturing planner, and I just took it from there. I love the electronics industry with its new technologies and innovation. We all take different journeys, and it's neat to see it's not always about a university education. It's sometimes just about being resilient.

I like the word persevere because that's what I do. At times you just want to give up, but you have to put perseverance to work and keep going. Drive and focus

*Canda is the VP Global Channel Sales of TE Connectivity*

*Canda*

# The Power of the Network

Nine out of 10 women I speak to about building their network say, "I know I need to network, but I don't have time." Or, as Kathleen Valentine, GM, Prescription Drug Monitoring & Toxicology at Quest Diagnostics, said, "I have always recognized, intellectually, the benefit and value of networking. I just didn't do it. I didn't make it a priority. My priority was my family and my work, and you just keep plugging away. Knowing how valuable having and establishing a network can be, I always got it, but I never did it."

**Network** (noun)
1. Strategic asset
2. **Network = Net Worth**

When I use the word network, I'm not referring to the verb "networking," the dreaded extracurricular activity and time commitment many women duck for the slightest reason. The fact is that women often see networking as an activity done after 5 p.m., or as a distraction from their job and family. Most of the women I have interviewed lament that this was the main reason they fell short on building their networks. And they cite that as detrimental to their career.

As Julie Fasone Holder, CEO and Founder of JFH Insights, says, her tenure in the C-suite of a Fortune 500 company was the loneliest time in her life, and the most challenging — because she had not built the relationships that she needed for her support structure. She left her role earlier than she had planned (see Julie's story on page 156).

"I didn't have people around me who were rooting for me. It was extremely lonely at the top, and the support systems that existed before were nonexistent."

As you move up in your career, your relational skills are key to staying at the top of your game. Early in your career, you are building credibility with your technical expertise, but by the time you are in a management position, you should be pulling on those relational skills to develop connections with your senior executives, your peers, your colleagues, and your employees.

Your network is an asset; a strategic asset and a necessary one. But if you approach it like it's a root canal — a necessary evil, you will miss the boat. The network I am talking about is the set of relationships that is there for you through thick and thin, providing you relevant and usable information to keep your career healthy. But it is not just about business excellence. Done well, the network also makes your personal life easier. Yes, easier. And richer.

# Pam Kimmet

## Change is energizing. Regularly 're-potting' yourself in to new situations helps you grow.

One of the mistakes I made early in my career was believing that all that mattered was the work I produced. I was naïve and thought that meeting my commitments meant I was a good team member, and that I would be recognized and successful for doing what was asked of me. Don't get me wrong, knowing your stuff and getting things done is very important to being successful, but I came to learn that what was equally important is to build strong, genuine relationships.

I got lucky and was given a role that I didn't really want, but it required me to interface with people across the company.

I quickly came to see the value — personally and professionally — of building trusted relationships. I learned more, did better work, got more done, and felt so much more connected ... and I had more fun and built enduring friendships.

And it opened doors to me for roles thereafter that I really wanted and likely wouldn't have been considered for without having built this network of supporters.

*Pam is the Chief Human Resources Officer of Cardinal Health*

**When asked, "Who can be a reference for you?," it's important to recognize that it is not about who you know, but who really knows you.**

It really helps to have a portfolio of people whose judgment you respect, and with whom you can be vulnerable and ask for help when you are stuck and not sure what to do, or advice on how to navigate a situation. Because the one thing no one tells you is that if you achieve your ambitions and move in to higher leadership roles, you will find it can be very lonely. Your team and others come to you for direction and solutions, and even though leadership today is supposed to be about helping the group find collective wisdom to determine what to do, there are many moments when you have to "pick the lane" and make a call on the path forward. Having some trusted advisors and friends with whom you can talk openly is key to your success … and your sanity!

**When you can be comfortable in your own skin, you're always at your true, full power.**

I am of the generation of women who felt like they needed to wear silky ties and suits that were versions of menswear in order to legitimize ourselves as professionals. In talking with a group of younger women a while back, they looked at me with stunned faces when I recounted some stories of what it was like, not that long ago, and spoke of how things had evolved for women over my career. All of us — men and women — can be caught in the trap of trying to project and "be" someone that we really are not. I can honestly say that when I learned to stop doing that, to be willing to let myself come through, I was not only happier, but I was also more impactful in

what I did. This is not to suggest that I deflect feedback and don't constantly strive to be a better version of myself. But it is to say that I have learned that being real is so important. Understanding this about yourself is then connected to knowing what environments you want to be in and who you want to work with.

Think about who you are and what you want, when presented with job opportunities. Don't be drawn in to an opportunity just because the company is well-known and considered a leader in its field; make sure it's a place you would be really happy and want to be. Even if the role or company seems to be exactly what you want, be honest with yourself and those you meet, in terms of how you approach the interviewing process. Don't pretend to be someone, or respond to them in inauthentic ways, to get the offer. Really assess if you want to work with the people you meet; make sure you learn all you need to about the organization to make sure it fits you. Don't fall into the trap of thinking you can make it work, or that you should go for it because of the company's reputation … or, worse, to simply leave where you are currently.

# Relationships Inside Your Company: Remaining a Top Performer

Inside the organization, you are likely to be working with a fairly consistent group of individuals. It is easy to stay heads down and just "do your job." But when you become an executive leader, the "job" is no longer just the "doing." It is about creating great working relationships with the *right* people.

Rob Cross, a professor at the University of Virginia's McIntire School of Commerce, has studied the impact of networks on leadership success for nearly 20 years. What's interesting to learn from his work is that the top performers who remain top performers do so because of the networks they keep. Top performers build networks that tie them into other parts of their organization. They build relationships across functions, across roles, and across geographies.[2]

Further, the approach these top performers take to relationship-building is not about running around the organization tapping people for their network value, but rather **they create "pull" because of the enthusiasm and energy they bring to their job. That "pull" opens up opportunities and avenues to new talent and extends the network naturally.**

This is *NOT* a numbers game. It's not about how many people you know; it's about who you know and the quality of the relationships you create with them.

## Start with Awareness

I once tried a simple exercise with a group of 30 CEOs. I asked them to list the five critical relationships they needed to have in order for them to be successful, and then rate the strength of each relationship on a five-point scale. Almost every executive rated at least two of those five relationships as very weak.

That exercise created an awareness in the group that **relationships don't just happen because people are in close proximity to each other — even if you're the CEO.** You need to be intentional about building them.

In doing this exercise with many groups over the past few years, I've found that when a relationship falls on the lower end of the scale, it is typically one of two types: it is either a new relationship that needs to be cultivated, or an existing relationship that needs to be fixed. Either can be harmful. Those troubling relationships not only rob you of energy, they also create tension because communication isn't that easy and misunderstandings occur. That affects others and impacts their results, as well.

Relationships involve people, and dealing with people is not an exact science. There will be times when you find that a work relationship is rocky and it needs fixing. You need to figure out why it's not working and address those causes. I've found that the most common sources of problems in work relationships are:

* **People's perceptions of us precede us.** Before you even arrive in your new role or location, aspects of your reputation are shared with the new team. The positive aspects still have to be proven through words and actions, but the negative ones are assumed until they are corrected;

🌸 **Long-standing misunderstandings and differences can fester.** You can sometimes be at fault when you make assumptions about what others meant, or intended, or felt in a certain situation. Those assumptions can color your thinking and your perceptions. It's very easy to play the blame game and lay fault on the other person. The relationship spirals downward from there, and just gets worse over time; and

🌸 **We don't want to know each other.** Like it or not, sometimes you have to work with a person you just don't like. There may be no rational reason behind your feelings. It could be a physical attribute that reminds you of someone you didn't like before. Or maybe you find their style irritating. Whatever the reason, you convince yourself that you just don't want to know them, and therefore, do not engage.

When underlying relationship problems exist, it is better to meet them head on. Don't worry. You don't have to become best friends or invite them out to dinner. But you are in business, and your job requires you to relate to others in such a way that helps — not hinders — the success of that business. **When you intentionally address the mistaken perceptions, hidden assumptions, and inexplicable dislikes in your "difficult" work relationships, you clear these elephants from the room.** You make everyone more comfortable and create space for much better understanding and much easier collaboration.

# Successful leaders continue to be successful with the help of sponsorship within their companies

**98.5%** of leaders have at least 1 sponsor. Successful leaders don't hitch their wagon to one star.

*The bigger your base of sponsorship, the greater your opportunities for success.*

**63%** of successful leaders surveyed have at least 3 sponsors.

*SOURCE: Survey of 60 Executives from The Signature Program*

# Sonya Roberts

*I like to play on teams that like to win. Although I can appreciate a pretty game, if you lose there are no asterisks on the scoresheet.*

I grew up as an athlete in a family of athletes. I like to win, and I like to be on the winning teams. I get a rush out of working with people who like to win. I don't understand teams that play to not lose, or those that are satisfied with simply a pretty game. Although I can appreciate a pretty game, if you lose there are no asterisks on the scoresheet. Therefore, I firmly believe, as a leader, you can expect pretty games AND a favorable score.

## It's Not About the Next Job

I was raised in Minnesota and couldn't wait to leave for college. So I applied to schools outside of the Midwest and landed in Texas. Upon graduation, I ended up in the oil and gas industry and spent my first 19 years with the same company. They knew me well and I trusted them, so when job opportunities were presented, there was never a question about taking them. I moved nine times in those 19 years to different roles and various cities, including New Orleans, Houston, Anchorage, and even Stavanger, Norway. I trusted their vision about my career because of that long-term relationship, so every time

*Sonya is the President of Cargill Growth Ventures & Strategic Pricing, Cargill Protein of Cargill*

I got the call, I went. When I came to Cargill, it was the first time that I actually applied for a job.

I wanted to come back home to Minnesota, and Cargill was a great option for me. I joined in energy and moved to the salt business a year later. What was different was that I didn't have the longstanding relationships, so when Cargill offered me the role in the egg business several years later, I needed to give it some thought. I was not any less driven or aspirational, but it was no longer about the "next job." The decision needed to factor in if it was a good fit for me — the team I would be working with, the leadership, and the health of the business. Being in a role that is not a good fit can consume a lot of energy. I'd rather expend my energy on the people, building a winning team, and the market, than working through the noise of a bad fit.

**I'm at a point in my life where it's not just about passing through jobs. This is about what I want to do and representing who I am.**

## Know Your Values

I firmly believe in knowing your values because they show up in your leadership. Respect for others is one of my top three values (along with relationships and health). **I genuinely believe every single person is special to someone and deserves to be treated with respect.** I remember being with my grandmother as a little girl, and I thought she hung the moon. To the world, however, she was an uneducated, unmarried black woman in Mississippi, working blue-collar jobs and, as a result, was not always treated with great respect. I certainly didn't understand the dynamics of the discrimination she was living — quite honestly, I'm not sure I fully understand it today, but I did know she was very important to me and I wanted everyone to be nice to her. If you ever want to see me mad at someone, it generally has to do with them being disrespectful to others. You will remember that conversation.

*Sonya*

## Building Your Courage Muscle

I consider courage to be like any other muscle that you have to develop and continue to build over time. You have to take little steps along the way that lead to the bigger steps. **I wish I had started standing up for who I am earlier in life. If I had done that in small increments, inside and outside of work, then I could've built that muscle earlier, and it would have showed up when I needed it most.**

Right after the birth of my second daughter, a group of friends enticed me to run a marathon, even though I am not a runner. They trained me through the whole process. It took little victories along the way to finally reach the big day. When the marathon day came, the group went together, but my training friends were all running the half marathon, so our starting lines were in different places. As I split off and walked over to the starting line for the marathon, I stopped on the side of the road and began to cry. I didn't know anybody, and I was starting to doubt myself.

When I gained my composure, I saw someone holding a sign with the number "6" on it and saw a small group of runners convening in that area. I couldn't believe there were only six-minute milers in the marathon (especially considering I'm a 10-plus-minute miler) and it was all starting to get to my head. When I asked the sign holder about the "6," he replied, "This is for the six-hour marathoners!" What a sigh of relief. As I moved up the road to my sign, I started to realize, I have done the preparation and I need to stop worrying. Once I completed the race, my courage muscles were on overdrive. Since then, **I have run other races (marathons included) and become quite bold about trying new things. Those muscles keep getting stronger and stronger.**

# Q How do you go about fixing difficult relationships?

**Shanna Wendt:** I try to approach difficult relationships from a place of optimism. No one's trying to be difficult, and no one's trying to have a bad day or to make it more problematic. I try getting behind what their drivers are, or what is motivating them, or what perspective they're coming from. For those more challenging that I can't figure out, I call upon other relationships in my network to help me see them from a different perspective.

—Shanna Wendt, VP of Communications | Coca-Cola European Partners

**Jenny Cormack-Lendon:** I used to think that when I had a difficult relationship with somebody at work, it was because they didn't like me. This would often upset, even offend me.

So I started to think differently about my working relationships. The reason we have good personal relationships is because we put a lot of time, energy, and effort into them. Work relationships are no different. You will have a natural chemistry with some people, and it is therefore much easier to form a good working relationship with them. Other relationships will be difficult. You are never going to be the best

of friends, but you do need to work productively together. I used to avoid these people or remain quiet in meetings with them. However, I have learned to actively see how that person spends time, gotten to know them, and, more importantly, allowed them to get to know me. People can relate to those who they know better, and the end result is a better working relationship.

—Jenny Cormack-Lendon, Supply Chain Director, Cargill Agricultural Supply Chain, EMEA | Cargill

**Canda Carr:** When you find it difficult to connect with someone, you can't take it personally. It's usually about business and the workplace. If you take time to truly understand what matters to people, or what motivates them, you have a better chance of finding a way to connect with them and bring mutual value to moving things in a positive direction. Because I am a competitive person, I often challenge myself to win people over, and I usually win.

—Canda Carr, VP Global Channel Sales | TE Connectivity

One executive in our program admitted that she had a colleague that she had to work closely with and she just didn't like him. She couldn't explain it, but the mere instant he was in the same room, she did not want to engage and did not like their interactions. As we talked about how to change this, I suggested she consciously approach their next interaction with one goal only: find out something personal about him. Several months later, when I asked how it was going, she relayed a wonderful outcome. "I found out we had several things in common. His daughter actually lives in my neighborhood, and he grew up not far from where I grew up. Then each time I saw him, we began to uncover more common things, and now when I ask him about his family, I am genuinely interested in his answer. It has made working together totally different."

## Relationships Improve as Trust Goes Up

You may be wary of showing vulnerability in the business world. But it can be so powerful when you do, because it increases trust. And you don't necessarily have to get into the "deep" stuff. It can be as simple as asking about someone's interests or sharing a bit of information about yourself, as you discovered reading Kathleen Valentine's story in Chapter One (pg 34). She learned that sharing a story about her family and their importance in her life could change how she was perceived in her organization.

As many of the stories in this book illustrate, the more you share vulnerability, the more that people trust you. And as trust grows, the connections become deeper and richer.

## Never Let a Colleague Fail

A colleague and I were both being considered as candidates for the same role. We became great buds during the eight months of our assessment period. We had a common purpose, we valued each other, we resonated in how we worked, and we were a winning team. But as soon as I was fortunate to be named to the role, something changed, and our relationship shifted and drifted. The other individual was offered a great role within the company, but his passion was still in HR.

**Neither of us were our authentic selves, and I began to doubt myself. For three months, we went through this separately.**

Finally, we sat down together over a great dinner and decided to open up with one another. We explored what we were really feeling. As soon as we had the courage to be that vulnerable with each other, we realized that we both still had positive intent, incredibly strong values, and valued each other's contributions. We had been misinterpreting, and reading in between the lines, because of our own insecurities and self-doubts. With that discovery, we were able to partner back up again and commit to each other's successes. Then it was all about how we could win together for our new company and our associates, going forward.

When we allow ourselves to be vulnerable, and human, and express what we feel, it makes a big difference to the people we work with, to the people we impact, and to ourselves.

**Abbe Luersman**
Chief Human Resources Officer | Ahold Delhaize

# Cecile Thaxter

> ## Communication is one of those fascinating things, where it's really about your audience and their frames of reference.

I am Jamaican by birth, so the Bob Marley song that says, "One love, one heart, let's get together and feel all right," has been a great theme for me because love stands for unity.

### Yes, love.

Running a mining operation was a new role for me and very different from anything I had ever done. Having a female leader who came out of business finance was new and very different for the operation, as well. Prior to coming here, I thought I was a pretty strong communicator.

### After a few months in my new role, I realized I was not communicating as well as I'd thought. I looked behind me, but no one was there.

*Cecile is the General Manager of Newmont Mining Corporation.*

I took a lot of things for granted, such as organizational effectiveness and leadership. But we were not there. I had to stop, listen, learn, and adapt. I started meeting one-on-one with employees at all levels to make it personal and to understand backgrounds and interests. Understanding an individual's experiences and triggers, explaining "why," as well as choosing the right words, are critical to effective communication.

I never thought of myself as a creative person, but I have had to become creative when communicating. There are different ways to reach people, so I tried to find new and exciting ways to make that work — incorporating quizzes, stories, models, pictures, and even songs **(sometimes accompanied by dance)** to make interactions more enjoyable.

What I'm doing now is one of the most challenging, demanding, exciting, enlightening, and (more importantly) fun and rewarding things I've ever done. I've learned that despite the fact that my people are "hardcore" miners, at the end of the day, we are all humans.

**We all want to be understood, and we all want to understand.** We are more similar than different, and that message is integral to my "Yes, love" theme.

All of this improved communication has fostered a lighter, friendlier, and more productive environment.

*Cecile*

> *Building a network is the single, most powerful tool to accelerate success for any individual or organization.*
>
> Cielo Hernandez
> VP and CFO of North America | Maersk Line

# The Power of Connection

My daughter and I choose books to read together and discuss our reflections on them. While talking about my business and how I believe that a person's network equals their net worth, my daughter shared something she had recently read. **"When it comes to relationships, no interaction is net-neutral."** I stopped talking. Here's a young woman who has never worked in the business world sharing this wisdom with me, but she was right.

Virtually every interaction you have with another person moves the needle toward either the positive or the negative. Sometimes it moves a little bit; sometimes a lot. Whether you are speaking with someone in the board room or in the checkout line of the grocery store, you are adding to, or subtracting from, the relationship. You need to be aware of how you are impacting your relationships with every opportunity you are given to shape them.

## The Power of One Word

Words are so powerful that it doesn't take many of them to have an impact. As a leader, you have to be conscious about how your words are being heard. Just a few misinterpreted words can have unintended consequences. It can be a lot like tossing a pebble in a pond and producing ripples in all directions. A CEO of a global telecom company once told me of a lesson he learned about this. During his first 30 days in his new role at the top of the company, he emailed a question to one of his direct reports on a Friday. It was nothing urgent. But that executive and five others on his team worked the entire weekend to come up with an answer by Monday. The CEO had had no intention of causing this effect, but his simple words were like throwing a pebble in the pond, with significant impact on others.

One word can also impact your connection with others. Words of encouragement or a quick acknowledgment lift people up. Small gestures can change the entire dynamic in the room. I worked for a CEO who would give out $2 bills to employees on the spot. As he walked down the hall, he might stop an individual and recognize them for something they had done a week ago. It wasn't about the $2; it was about the words he conveyed in 15 seconds. Even the VPs displayed their $2 bills in their offices to remind them of the conversations. Meaningful words and gestures move the relationship needle in a positive direction, and the impact can't be overstated. Long after you are out of their lives, people will remember how you made them feel.

# Maria Blasé

One thing that brings me great joy is giving people meaningful work so they can support their families, so they can develop and grow, and so they can become productive members of their communities. I want to give this to others, and I want it for myself as well.

**Men are promoted on potential, women on performance. If a man doesn't perform well in a new role, then it's "the role doesn't fit." With a woman, what's next might be "out."**

*Maria is the President, HVAC and Transport Latin America of Ingersoll Rand*

*Take risks, but don't be afraid to ask for the ability to not let it become an up or out.*

I remember how this played out when a CFO offered me a promotion into a role that I knew would partly be a turnaround. There was a lot of work to be done. I also knew that making a jump across functions, or across businesses, may represent an even bigger risk for a woman than for a man.

So I asked for a safety net. I said, "I'm willing to take this risk. I want to take it. But this is my career, and I want you not to forget my whole career because of this one next role. Will you let me return to finance if this role doesn't work out? Will you take me back?" They said yes, and I accepted the job.

Turnarounds take time — and patience. By the end of the first five months, I realized that it would take nine months to a year. That meant I would have to have enough patience to hang in there and do what needed to be done. And my boss would need to know this was something I could handle. So I had a conversation with him in which both of us got a lot of things on the table, including our frustration about what we saw was happening. It went a long way towards getting us on the same page and building on the trust we already had. A year later, even though we were not entirely making the numbers (due, in part, because of external circumstances beyond our control), he was complimenting me on the performance of the team — and my performance as well.

*Maria*

# Q

# When you are in the C-suite, how is your impact like a pebble in the pond?

**Joanne Bauer:** Everything you do, people watch. One day I was walking over to our cafeteria, which is in another building on the campus, thinking. My day was booked all day long and so, when I walked over to lunch, that was the only time I could think. When I got back from lunch, someone told me, "Something must be wrong because you weren't smiling on your way to lunch." I said, "Wow, that is an amazing piece of feedback. Nothing is wrong, I was just thinking about something." Their response was, "Well, quit thinking and just smile." I thanked them and made sure that, when I walk over to lunch now, I smile and say hello to people.

—Joanne Bauer, retired President Health Care | Kimberly-Clark Corporation

**Marcia Avedon:** While the work is very fulfilling, it is also something I take very seriously. Everyone is watching and listening to you. Whether you like or not, you are now a model for the organization. One inappropriate, off-the-cuff remark — even in an informal situation — can reverberate across the organization and, depending on who you are and your company's visibility, can be picked up by the media. You have to be keenly sensitive to all the messages you're sending, both verbal and non-verbal, all the time.

—Marcia J. Avedon, SVP Human Resources, Communications, and Corporate Affairs | Ingersoll Rand

**Teri McClure:** When I got to the senior team, my predecessor told me that people are reading everything you do. Every morning, our entire senior team that sits on the same floor heads down to breakfast together at 7:30. We do that again at lunchtime, always sitting in the same area. It's like clockwork. She told me that everyone in the cafeteria watches us to see if we are smiling, or talking, or laughing, and people are reading everything that we do.

You don't realize, as a senior executive, just how the little things that you do or say can cause ripple effects, in terms of people responding to them. If I were to say in a meeting, "I don't like something anymore," such as the use of a word, the next thing you might hear is, "Teri said you absolutely can't use this word anymore."

—Teri McClure, Chief Human Resources Officer and SVP Labor Relations | United Parcel Service of America, Inc.

# Sharon Johnson

*I'm much more likely to face into a problem versus focusing on the reasons why it's going to be difficult.*

have a serious health issue — it causes you to realize life is too short.

As far as the impact on my career — and my life — it pulled me to focus on the things that I could control and influence. I will focus on what needs to be done and get on with it. I find I'm much more positively orientated to challenges than I was before. My advice to anyone is, don't wait for life to teach you that lesson.

Focusing on my strengths and telling myself that I don't have to be anything other than who I am, that's where my successes come from.

When I began defining my signature, my reflections revealed that I'm really a problem-solver. Every time I've made a career move, it's been to address an issue, make a change, drive improvement, or change the outcome for the team, the business, or our customers. Too often, people try to anticipate what they believe the workplace wants from them, and then try to fit into that. I think that causes a lot more personal stress and pressure that hinders your effectiveness.

You have to give yourself permission to be true to yourself, to work through your own values, and to encourage others to be successful.

I had a health issue and was under treatment for the better part of a year — a watershed moment in my life. At the time I didn't want it to be a career interruption, although it was a life interruption, so I essentially kept working while I was on chemo and undergoing treatment. It was a bit crazy then, but on reflection, it was a coping mechanism for me as well, although I think I'd deal with it differently now. As too often happens in life, when traumatic experiences happen — you lose somebody or

*Sharon is the SVP Quality, Product Development & Regulatory Affairs of Catalent, Inc.*

# How to Build Relationships that Work

We need to be intentional about building relationships. One way to do that is to adopt several relationship-building techniques that have been proven to work over time.

**Prepare to relate.** Review as much information as you can, ahead of time, about the person you are meeting. Look people up on LinkedIn and note what interests they have listed, what schools they went to, and what they look like. Seek out information from others who already have a relationship with them to find out more about their interests, desires, and even their interaction style. Having relevant data makes finding points of connection easier, and it will increase your confidence when you're interacting with someone who is no longer a total "stranger."

**Aim to connect.** My son's baseball coach had a great approach to getting started. He told the boys that when they go up to bat, their job is to just "get the bat on the ball." They are not to swing for the fences and try to hit a home run on the first pitch. Just focus on connecting the bat to the ball. The same applies to relationships. If you're tense or uncertain about building rapport with an executive who is senior to you, remember that most leaders enjoy being asked about their opinions and experiences. You might open the door with a request to learn more about their perspective over a quick cup of coffee outside the formal work environment.

**Build equity over time.** Building a relationship is like building up a bank account. You start making small investments, and eventually you end up with a healthy balance that allows you to make withdrawals. For each relationship, whether it's brand new or in need of improvement, begin with a small goal that can start to move it in the direction you want to go. Then keep investing small "deposits" of yourself over time to build your relationship equity.

**Listen like you mean it.** In today's world, multi-tasking seems to be the norm. Yet people know when you are not listening and not fully present with them. This can have disastrous consequences in your relationships, especially in global environments where you must rely on virtual connections. Make a point of focusing on the person(s) in front of you, whether you are with them face-to-face or via technology. Stop answering emails and texts. Stay in the conversation at hand.

# Beth O'Brien

## Whenever you're facing a big challenge, believe in yourself.

Growing up, I would drop by her house on the way home from school each day and we would spend time chatting. Her door was always open. Her two sisters, my 60- and 70-year-old great-aunts, had both been in the Army and often came to visit her. All three women would cast their pearls of wisdom my way.

Angel Mom gave me three pearls. First, she taught me to **believe in myself**, that I had a good brain in my head, and that if I worked hard and was persistent, I could do anything that I wanted. She did tell me that, depending on what path I chose, it would be a little bit harder for me as a woman.

She also taught me to **think for myself**. She knew the power of listening and would ask me very thoughtful questions that helped me think through and process things. I learned from her how to help others think through their challenges and opportunities.

Lastly, she taught me the **importance of family and laughter**. Angel Mom loved to cook. She would make meals and invite the family over, and we'd sit down at that dinner table and linger for hours, just chatting and laughing.

Her three pearls of wisdom were valuable during my most recent career transition. When my position was eliminated, I kept reminding myself to believe all I had to do was use great questions to think my way through and select which opportunity was my right next step. I'm excited to step into my new role because I know I have a lot to offer and a lot to learn from all the people with whom I'll be meeting, working, and hopefully, sometimes laughing.

When your job is eliminated, you have to remember it's not about you or your performance. It's a business decision. Especially at times like this, you have to keep believing in yourself.

During those challenging teenage years, my paternal grandmother (nicknamed Angel Mom) was my greatest influence. She lived just two blocks away from us, and I watched my strong sage of a grandmother struggle with ovarian cancer. The doctors told her she was only going to live two or three years; she turned that into eight. To this day, I still draw on the gifts she gave me.

*Beth is the Head of Enterprise Program Management Office of T. Rowe Price*

*E. M.*

## Phone Call Fridays

**It's important to be connected to what's going on in a company.** The more connected you are, and the more you know what's going on, the more you can bring the voice of the company into your discussions and decisions. I have a two-hour commute to get home on the weekends. I do what I call "phone call Fridays." I'm just dialing different people along the drive to see what's going on in their businesses. **Being a person who knows what's going on is incredibly helpful.**

**Joan Wainwright**
President, Channel and Customer Experience | TE Connectivity

## Embedding Relationship Building into Your Life

We need to be aware and intentional about building and growing relationships. Intentionality can be as easy as making the most of otherwise "dead" time. That's what Joan Wainwright, President of Channel and Customer Experience at TE Connectivity, does with her commute time.

With an intentional view to making connections, Tina Tromiczak, SVP of Global Business Solutions at ADP, walks through company facilities, twice a day, to talk to employees face-to-face.

"I get really concerned when my voice is too far away. When your voice has to go filtering through several layers, it's like that telephone game. Your message never hits the floor the same way you started it."

# Relationships Outside Your Company: Gaining Diverse Perspectives

A leader typically succeeds by bringing ideas and strategic thinking to the organization. Today, those insights have to be especially nimble, current, and fresh. Relationships that reach beyond the boundaries of your company can be a rich source of that kind of information. An external network can keep you connected to a changing world.

It can also help you stay grounded and see past the erroneous assumptions you can make when you are too close to a situation.

Additionally, an external network can expand the pool of people who can advocate on your behalf and help you navigate through challenges, perhaps helping you to prepare for an interview, or work through a sticky local government issue, or even just find a dentist in a new city. In short, it gives you a broader base of support.

# Sue Liddie

*The price of poker goes up, the higher you go up the ladder, but a support structure is important no matter where you are.*

I've always had the theory that if I didn't love what I was doing, I should do something else ... and that if I was loving it, then I should make sure I was making a difference.

I love the work that I do. I love working for a company that's mission-based. I love working in an environment where it's making a difference for women. I love technology; it's what my entire career has been about. I love seeing us build things that make a difference for the people that use our products. And I actually enjoy leading teams to a place that brings them satisfaction and that delivers on capabilities that a company desperately needs.

In the early days of your career, you think you can conquer the world, and that you don't need a lot of relationships or help from a network. That is a complete fallacy! When you are faced with adversity or uncertainty, you need a close group of people that can guide you through.

I learned, later than I wished, the value of relationships, and networks, and ensuring you have support around you — both inside and outside your company. Years ago, I lost a job because I hadn't worked my internal network. I didn't have a support

*Sue is the Group VP and Chief Information Officer of Avon Products, Inc.*

system to protect me when a new leader came in. Fortunately, I bounced back in a big way, and I ended up in a better place after that wake-up call. But the lesson learned was not to underestimate the value of relationships.

It doesn't matter how many above-average performance reviews you have had, if you aren't working your broader relationships, it can all change in a New York minute.

Building a network is hard work. It is intentional work. Sometimes this takes courage. I'm naturally more of a wallflower. Walking into a one-on-one is hard work for me. Over time, you develop the skills and a playbook that works.

Now I schedule time with my peers across the organization, with managers who are above me and with key high potentials that are coming up in the ranks. I spend time planning, setting an agenda, and thinking through how I can be helpful to the other person. Because every one of those relationships will have an influence, at some point in time.

I also have a personal board of advisors. They comprise a diverse set of perspectives, ideas, and experiences — and they care about me as a person. When I moved to my CIO role, they were the best prep for my transition to working with a public board of directors.

These jobs don't end when you leave the office or get to 5 p.m. on Friday. I also have all of the right support systems in my personal life to help me create the additional capacity I need to stretch it, beyond when I'm in the office. It has made all the difference to have a long-term relationship with a partner who truly feels that part of his role is to do what he can to help me have a good day. If I'm having a good day, everybody around me is having a good day.

No one in my support structure is threatened by who I am, what I have achieved, or what I'm still looking to accomplish. They build and sustain my energy. They give me enthusiasm around the things that, day-to-day, each and every one of us need to tackle. I feel like they are my personal cheering squad. They boost my energy to tackle the tough things.

Support is encouragement. Support is the circle of people around me that helps me understand the art of the possible, not just for what I'm doing, but for what I'm trying to accomplish with the teams I'm leading.

*Sue*

# best advice
## from a mentor

I had one tough boss who set standards very high, but was equally okay if you did not get it right the first time. He used a baseball analogy: even the best players who are hitting .300 miss seven out of 10 times. Not that you *want* to miss seven out of 10 times, but as long as you're taking time out to reflect on each missed hit, **as long as you're improving, as long as you're learning, as long as you're bringing a better game the next day, that's part of what leading is all about.**

# Three Types of External Networks

I think of external relationship networks as falling into three types: your *constellation*, your *board of advisors*, and your *posse*.

## Your Constellation

The constellation network is all about having access to a wide array of people who have expertise and knowledge that you might need. They probably won't be your close friends, but having access to them can change how you are viewed inside your company. Every time you go into a meeting of your leadership, you should go prepared to share a point of view on one agenda item that is outside of your domain. You don't have to have an opinion on it, but you can share insight that might advance the discussion or provide fresh thinking inside the room. Kristie Dolan, General Manager of Women's Health at Quest Diagnostics, did exactly this. As her company considered an acquisition where they had to create a stand-alone P&L, she reached out to a senior leader she knew at another company who had done something similar. She says:

> "I shifted my networking from 'me and my career' to 'it's about me winning in my job today.'"

When Katie Carter, VP of Human Resources at Hyatt, was asked to take a lateral position that would entail moving her family from Chicago to Hong Kong, she wasn't sure it was the right move. When she attended The Signature Program, I encouraged her to use her constellation network. She queried the other executives for their experiences on moving to new countries and taking lateral moves. She tapped into this constellation of perspectives to her advantage. It helped her make the right decision. Several years later, her family is thriving in Hong Kong, and she is benefiting from both personal and professional growth, along with an extended set of relationships inside her company (see Katie's story on page 128).

You can't know everything, but our constellation network can help you know a lot more and fill in gaps in your knowledge. Que Dallara, SVP of Corporate Strategy at TE Connectivity, says she has been consciously tapping into external sources, in part to address the fact that "I don't know what I don't know." "A while back," she recalls, "We needed information for a big data team I'm now responsible for, and I went looking for experts through my network outside the company, and even some cold calls, to gain perspective from others with similar roles. That helped me hone in on what to focus on, and made me feel comfortable that I was not missing something."

The network constellation is also a wonderful asset when you are deciding about your next career move. You might aspire to a certain role, but having a good understanding of what that role looks like on a day-to-day basis, or which challenges are inherent in that role, is difficult to see from afar. Abbe Luersman, CHRO of Ahold Delhaize, interviewed more than 20 C-suite executives that were either CHROs or CEOs to decide if this was the path she wanted to truly take (see Abbe's story on page 102).

> "Everything I learned through those interviews helped build my confidence that one day, when the right opportunity came up, I could be successful."

## *Your Personal Advisory Board*

The second tier of the external network is what I refer to as my personal advisory board. Public companies have boards of directors that provide the corporate leadership team with diverse sets of ideas, advice, and perspectives from outside the organization. Why shouldn't you have one? Think of it as a personal board of advisors for You, Inc.

Neither the leaders of a public company, nor you as CEO of You, Inc., can know everything you need to know to make the wisest decisions possible. A personal board of advisors can become a significant asset in your career if you know how to select, build, and tap into them for their wisdom, at the right moments. They can definitely help you along the way, and building one is not as difficult as you may think.

# Advice about Networking

Think positively about networking, because networking is refreshing. You learn by talking to people, and you always learn something. If everything you do is with this fear of what others may think about you, you'd just stop doing everything. You would stop having friends. But networking is like friendship; it's give and take. Start externally, if that is easier. Meet your peers in other companies, talk to your advisers, and talk to others in the same field. You will begin to create a habit that you can replicate in-house, and you're going to do that with a lot of passion, joy, and energy. You're going to realize how efficient it is, and it will develop your business, your skills, yourself, and others, too.

**Karine Uzan-Mercie**
**VP Tax and Strategic Corporate Initiatives | Coca-Cola European Partners**

# Julie Fasone Holder

*There may come a time when you go to a role for which you have no experiences to draw on that are helpful.*

When I was a junior in high school, my father lost his business and our home. I went from a comfortable middle-class existence to virtual poverty. My mother became the chief breadwinner and an inspiration to me. That profoundly shaped me and made me much more independent, ambitious, and resilient than many of my peers.

In 2004, I moved from the chemicals division of Dow, where I had spent 20 years, to the plastics division. Here, I would be leading 1,500 people while dealing with new businesses and a new business model. For a while during the transition, I worked with an executive coach. After doing an initial 360-review, he said to me, "You know, people don't know you or what you stand for." So he asked me to write down my personal credo, including how I wanted to lead and how I wanted to be known.

I came up with 10 bullet points about what was important to me (like *trust*), and what people could expect from me as a leader (like a commitment to make *them* successful). Then I had a communications person help me polish it up before I rolled it out to my leadership team. My leadership credo had an amazing impact.

*Julie is the CEO and Founder of JFH Insights*

The credo became an incredible alignment tool that made us all accountable to lead with a new set of behaviors.

I started hearing that people now understood what my expectations were. My direct reports started preparing their own credos and aligning them with mine. Then they started cascading the whole exercise down the organization. Sharing that one exercise effectively instilled a new culture of leadership in a historically hierarchical organization.

## Unmet Expectations

Of course, the credo didn't mean that everyone's expectations were always met. One expectation I had, for instance, went unmet when I moved into the C-suite. I moved into the C-suite role thinking that I had been sufficiently trained and prepared for it through my 32 years of experience with the organization. I was a good leader, and I was smart. I knew how to run organizations. I knew how to lead. I was ready.

Those three years in the C-suite were the hardest of my career. For me, life at the top was very different and very lonely.

That really surprised me. I just assumed that I could do things the way I had always done them because my previous experiences had helped me succeed in the past.

In hindsight, I realized that I didn't have a great appreciation for two things:

One, I knew there were differences between running a function and running a business, but I didn't appreciate the differences in the value the company saw between the two. I was used to running businesses. My background was in marketing, sales, and business leadership. The C-suite role was about running functions: HR, public affairs, and marketing and sales for the entire company. Having someone with business skills like myself running these functions meant I would inevitably be inviting people to look at things differently than they had in the past (i.e., from the perspective of how are we supporting the businesses).

Two, I didn't think strategically about the importance of allies. I approached the role the same way I had done all the rest of the jobs in my career, which was in terms of working together to try to build a really good organization.

I didn't have people around me who were rooting for me. The support systems that existed before were nonexistent.

I was fairly naïve about how politics and "insiding" worked at the top and how protective people would be of their turf. I didn't understand the dynamics of working with my peers and the challenging nature of the culture. It was more competitive than any of my previous experiences.

No one was negotiating the conflicts in the "white space" to help us collaborate. Admittedly, some decisions I made probably should've been more thought through. Eventually, it got to the point where I didn't feel valued or valuable. I struggled a lot with that, as you might imagine.

# FAQs

## on Building the Board of Advisors for You, Inc.

### Who should be on your Board?

People who know you well, know how you process things, and who have no hesitation in giving you honest feedback. People who care about, and are invested in, you and your career. Exactly who *they* are will depend on where you are in your career. Match areas where you have less knowledge or capability with former colleagues or bosses, coaches, siblings, professors, even friends of friends who can help you fill those gaps because of their backgrounds or current roles. Bear in mind that your needs, like that of a business, are dynamic and will evolve. Over time, your board members will change. For example, if you are in a steep growth curve with your career or business, one particular board member with similar experiences may be extremely valuable. Later, you may be going through a period of M&As and not find their perspective as essential.

### How many Advisors do you need?

There is no right answer to this question. Today, after a dozen years of cultivating my board, I have a dozen people who serve as my personal advisors. Adding one advisor per year is very easy. Creating an entire board overnight can be overwhelming and unrealistic. Go slow and add to your board when a new perspective becomes beneficial.

## How do you ask people?

*Suck in your gut, open your mouth and be prepared to hear "yes."* Know that you don't have to tell them you want them for your Board. If you know them well already, you may wish to simply say you have always valued their perspective and that, given where you are in your career, you would cherish the opportunity to set up a consistent and ongoing dialogue to share ideas that could be helpful to both of you.

## Can you ask people you don't know?

Of course. For people you don't know, the approach is similar. If you have been connected via a referral, you can start by telling them that your mutual connection always talks about the value of their conversations and thought you both would benefit from starting your own connection. Notice the intention is for the benefit to be mutual. This is not a one-way interaction. Your board members should get value from what you bring to the table as well.

## How often, and where, should you meet?

Quarterly and face-to-face are good guidelines. But it depends on each individual board member. The key is that you want to build a regular cadence to your interactions. You want to plan for them and schedule them into your calendar. You can always defer a meeting, but establishing an ongoing rhythm is critical for both sharing value and building the relationship.

## Do you ever bring your Board of Advisors together in one room?

You don't have to, but you can, if you wish. Sometimes the interaction between board members can help you brainstorm possibilities or illuminate and avoid costly mistakes. I never thought about this until I heard a talk from a CEO of a major consumer products company explain why he brought his advisors to his home for a weekend. He was in consideration for the role of CEO, and he needed to generate some strategic ideas for a turnaround. The strategy they formed later became the basis of his plan for the company as CEO. He marveled that, by bringing all of his advisors together, it gave him a wide variety of perspectives to inform his own decision making, which was one of his keys to success in the role. I believe one of the keys to his success was that his advisors knew him well; how he thought and what his values and non-negotiables were. That combination ensured his strategy was something he could execute and lead. Powerful!

# Kim Greene

## When making tough career decisions, follow your heart.

My father profoundly influenced me by giving me the gift of confidence. That gift has helped me throughout my career.

He never made me feel I couldn't do something. In fact, he had high expectations that I would get good grades and develop a strong work ethic, including doing chores at home, and participating in music and sports. I was expected to contribute, from a young age. As a family, we did a lot of camping, and I was fully engaged in helping pitch the tent, carry the gear, and chop and carry the wood. My father made me feel good about working hard and seeing the results of that work. Whenever I had a problem, or couldn't figure something out, he never made me feel as though I couldn't find the solution. He instilled in me the belief that I was more than capable and could do anything I set my mind to. My father not only helped guide and shape my moral standards, attitude toward work, and outlook on life, but it's because of him I attended and completed engineering school.

## Life doesn't always take the direction you thought, or intended. Be open-minded about change.

Having graduated with a Master's Degree in Biomedical Engineering, I planned to have a career designing artificial joints and limbs. I wanted to make

*Kim is the EVP and Chief Operating Officer for Southern Company*

people's lives better. Instead, 26 years ago I made the decision to accept a job with the power company, designing equipment for power plants. I quickly realized that the skills I developed as a biomedical engineer could be applied in a variety of disciplines. That was my first experience making a major change in my career path.

Since then, I have made several career changes, but the one constant has been my work in the energy industry. And while I didn't realize it when I accepted that first position, I have had the privilege of making people's lives better by helping to deliver a product — energy —that provides affordable comfort and convenience to the families we serve.

About 10 years ago, I was approached for an opportunity that was unexpected. The company happened to be headquartered in my hometown where my parents and in-laws live. In fact, it was the very company where my dad spent his entire career. I interviewed more for the learning experience, with no intention of accepting this new role if it were offered to me. When I was offered the role, I turned it down. The CEO said he would hold the position for me and asked that I take more time to consider. After a great deal of reflection, I realized this decision was not about me; it was about my family, and I needed to follow my heart. Being closer to my aging parents, and having my daughters develop strong relationships with their grandparents, aunts, uncles, and cousins was a wonderful gift in our lives. As it turned out, five-plus years at that company and three unique roles made me spread my wings and grow not only professionally, but also personally.

During this time away, I stayed in touch with my previous boss. Out of the blue, he called me and said, "It's time to come home." I let my heart lead the way again, and I returned. I love this company, this role, and the opportunities I have had. I particularly love that I have the chance to work with incredible female leaders as they evolve their own careers.

## Adjusting your leadership style is not about moving away from core strengths; it's about recognizing and discerning what is just simply not going to be effective.

The great thing about self-confidence, is I'm very comfortable making decisions on my own and moving forward quickly. And the bad thing about self-confidence is, I'm very comfortable making decisions and moving forward quickly. As a leader grows, it's important to be more collaborative and deliberate, to exhibit a certain level of gravitas; I have learned to adjust my style to be better in these areas.

*Kim*

# Release the Guilt!

### Have courage to pursue a career AND do what you love.

Ask for help when it's needed. Don't apologize. You don't have to be at every event for your child. When you are with your kids, give them the full attention they and you need. If you are happy, your children will be happy. When they see the passion and energy in what you do every day, they benefit and learn from that.

**Fill your board with individuals whose expertise and experience you need access to, but lack.**

Look for strong players who can act as sounding boards and challenge your thinking; who can freely give advice without being encumbered by organizational politics. That not only excludes current company colleagues, but also those who have recently left your company. You want executives who understand the shoes you walk in, but who aren't wearing the cloak of the company you are in. Most importantly, you want people who care for you personally, and for your success as a leader. They bring honest and open counsel to you.

"Creating a personal advisory board helps expand my views and provides me with another perspective. It gives me the opportunity to develop faster by learning from others," says Cielo Hernandez, VP and CFO of North America for Maersk Line. When she decided to create such a board, she recruited people who were in the types of roles that she aspired to. "I've been working in Finance and IT for over 24 years, and I wanted my next role to be a general manager," she explains. "As I assembled my board, I chose people who had achieved the success that I aspired to, such as presidents, CEOs, and commercial leaders.

## How I Created My Personal Board of Advisors

I was very intentional about reaching out to other CIOs and CHROs, both within the company and outside. It's more difficult to look around and figure out from whom you get advice within the organization. I can tell you, my personal board has served me very well and continues to, even today. Before I took my CIO role, I sought the advice of a number of those board members around "watch-outs" and what I should be focused on in the first 90 days. And recently, I faced a fairly large "bet-your-job" decision. I reached out to one of the CIOs to ask,

"Who are your advisors? Who would you suggest I talk to about this particular decision that I'm facing? Who can give me an external point of view and a more 360-degree lens around things that should be considered?"

**Sue Liddie**
Group VP and Chief Information Officer | Avon Products, Inc.

"It is critical to my personal growth and business development to know my strengths and weaknesses and surround myself with advisors who can fill these gaps."

Leaders with personal boards navigate the senior leadership challenges more readily. Read Sue Liddie's perspective in this section, or see her profile on page 152. She went after it with a vengeance and with wonderful outcomes. She was masterful, intentional, and methodical in her approach, and these new relationships have served her well.

Start building your board early in your career, if possible, or get started now. Just focus on one or two relationships for now, and build a regular cadence with these advisors.

Over several years, you will have built an asset that can be instrumental to your long-term success.

I have worked intentionally on building my own personal board for more than 15 years. Without that group of trusted, knowledgeable individuals, I wouldn't be where I am today. It surprised me, early in my career, how many people said "yes" when asked to be part of my personal advisory group. The scariest part was just asking.

# The Value of a Trusted Advisor

*I just can't tell you how important it is, as you go up the ladder, to have someone you can talk to whom you trust; someone who is objective, whose opinion you value, who will say to you, "You're a little out of line here," or "You absolutely have the right to do that. You're on the right track." I have a very close relationship with my husband. He's a wonderful man, sympathetic and supportive. But that doesn't help me solve my challenges at work. I need to call another trusted businesswoman and say, "This is what happened. This is what I'm thinking of doing. What do you think?" And they will give it to me straight, with the benefit of their experience and wisdom.*

**Jewelle Bickford**
Partner | Evercore Wealth Management

# Joanne Bauer

*I had to make sure I acted on the feedback they gave me to show them we were indeed creating a culture that was open and trusting.*

As I moved through my career, my mom was my sanity-check for helping me stay true to my beliefs and values. She was a stay-at-home mom in the 1950s, raising five children. She turned down a scholarship to the London School of Economics to marry and raise a family, but she profoundly influenced me in my business career. Whenever I had doubts, or was nervous about a big speech, she was on the other end of the phone, telling me all the reasons why I could do it.

I led the healthcare division of Kimberly-Clark. I was called in one day and told, "Well, your boss is no longer here, and you'll be taking over." I think I did okay. Women generally don't think they're ready. Maybe I wasn't ready, but I think it was actually a fairly good time.

It's harder than you think to go in as a new leader and just make the changes you want. Changing the culture was a lot more work than I expected, but it has been one of the most rewarding things I've done.

*Joanne is the former President Health Care of Kimberly-Clark Corporation*

Kimberly-Clark is a great 100-year-old-plus company with a strong culture and values focused on safety, employees, and customers. The healthcare division was in a different industry than the majority of the company. It grew through multiple acquisitions, and we needed to build on an already great culture to allow us to blend teams and cultures from multiple companies into one. Blending cultures into one built on trust was a focus for our team. It made it possible to have a debate — not an argument — in the room, and to give each other feedback that wasn't personally-based. You didn't have to agree with what we were doing, but you had to be aligned. The question if you weren't aligned was, what's it going to take to have you become aligned?

I told my deputy team that if we weren't modeling the behavior we wanted, then none of our employees would believe we were serious. We looked at the beliefs people held at each level in the organization and the beliefs we wanted them to hold. Primarily, they were around building trust and focusing on customers.

**I realized that I needed to be crystal clear on the vision, so that everybody could understand how their roles fit that, and then emulate the things we wanted in the culture, like feedback. I'd start every meeting with a story about something that showed the culture we wanted.**

People talked a lot about how hard feedback was. So, in an open meeting, I said, "I'll tell you what. Let's give *me* feedback." The whole room got quiet. I said, "That's great. That's feedback for me right there. So let's practice giving me feedback." By the end, they were. But I had to demonstrate to them that it wasn't necessarily about telling me something negative about myself. It was reinforcing, also, what they wanted to see more of, like me walking around the office more often.

**I think people want to work for a calm and confident leader — whatever gender that is; someone who brings order to the chaos.**

If you really want to lead an organization, you've got to be able to call out the reality, and the hope for the future, and really define those spaces for people. Then, everybody calms down.

*Joanne*

# A Great Partnership

One of the things that was hugely helpful to me was having a fabulous executive assistant, who was more of a partner than an assistant.

I had complete trust in her because she not only did her job well, but she took an active interest in the business. When you have someone that interfaces well, who has ownership in the business and wants to make it better, and is an extension of your brand, it makes for a great partnership.

## Your Posse

The third tier of your external networks is the innermost circle of people, at the core of your network.

There's an old adage: "Behind every successful man, there is a woman." I now believe that behind every successful woman, there is a posse!

Sandra Beach Lin, who sits on four Boards (American Electric Power, WESCO International, PolyOne Corporation, and Interface Biologics), introduced me to this concept. Think of your posse as the inner circle of people at the core of your network. These are the people who will be there for you through thick and thin, providing you with what's relevant and useful for keeping your career healthy, and making your personal life easier and richer.

Posse relationships are strong, enduring, and loving. They fuel your energy, your confidence, and your long-term health. They help you stay on track. They provide you with the straight talk you need to gracefully work through tough situations, and they advocate for you when you need someone in your corner.

**Posse relationships give you credible advice based on the fact that they know how you think, what is meaningful to you, and what lights you up.**

I recently got a call from someone in our Signature Network. Her first words were, "I have breast cancer." I could hear the loss of control in her voice. Female executives are great at solving problems. They tackle them with a step-by-step precision that moves them forward to a solution. But, put anyone in a situation that impacts them in a deep and personal way and they can forget how to respond. Lack of knowledge about what comes next can render anyone almost helpless.

"If everyone in your network looks like you, acts like you, and has your interests, how are you ever going to learn new things, discover new opportunities, or move in new directions?"

—Rob Cross[3]

> ## "The combination of a good friend you can talk to and the gym is magical."
>
> Jewelle Bickford
> Partner | Evercore Wealth Management

This is one of those times when calling on your posse can help.

### Having a posse changes your game — and your life — for the better.

I know many women who have successfully battled breast cancer and maintained their career trajectory. Once I found out where she wanted to receive treatment, I put a message out to people in our trusted network who lived or worked in those respective cities. Within 30 minutes, I had a dozen responses ranging from, "This is THE best doctor in this city," and "I know the head of oncology at this hospital and can arrange a phone call," to "I am available to walk through some selection criteria I missed when making this decision," and "Here are the questions that need to be on her list." That shared knowledge, that reassurance that others have "been there" before can help you see what your options are and how you might move forward. That's invaluable when you are facing anything for which you feel unprepared.

The value of relationships has played a significant role in the lives and careers of the women in these pages. The need for a learning network to keep fresh and relevant does not go away when we leave our full-time business roles. In fact, many of the stories in these pages are from women who have retired, and their networks still sustain them.

You can't go it alone, nor would I imagine you would want to. But often, you end up doing just that because you haven't taken the time to build those connections. I can tell you from experience that, once you get going, relationships grow exponentially. There is a wealth of learning to gain from so many varied connections.

Trusted connections help you see things that you would otherwise not have known about. They will make your business and personal lives richer.

# Jane Leipold

I grew up in the United States in a small town in the middle of Pennsylvania. My life has been quite different than many friends and family in my hometown. My career has taken me all over the world, from Brussels to Shanghai, from Germany to Brazil to Japan, and many more. Exploring and embracing opportunities to lead in a global business has been a wonderful learning experience.

I like to be challenged and make an impact. I like to be a part of change. I think people in the company who have known me for a long time would say I'm tough, persistent as hell, and true to my standards. I know I've changed over the years. It's never troubled me; in fact, I believe I have thrived!

*Jane is the retired SVP, HR of TE Connectivity*

## *I had to make myself more vulnerable when I got to the top job.*

I was with one company for 34 years and many have asked, "How could you stay that long?" Essentially, I have experienced more in one company than most have experienced in a career. I have had multiple careers — engineering, operations, and HR. My company was acquired by a major conglomerate, followed by a very public scandal creating a "near-death" experience, and then the company recovered. Finally, the company spun my business segment into a public company. You don't have to leave a company to gain valuable experience, achieve, and succeed.

**As I look back on my HR career, nobody in their right mind should have put me in the head of HR role, at the time. It was a big risk for me and the company. But I did think I could do it.**

I committed to make the place better again; a goal that was not easily achieved. I was not one to give up. Still, it was a much bigger challenge than I could have anticipated.

As you go through your career, you need to make decisions that are best for you, at that time of your life. Sometimes, though, sticking through some challenging times at your company can work out wonderfully well.

*Jane*

# Advice to My Younger Self

When I thought about networking in the past, it was always something I did "after hours." I needed to go to a dinner meeting, an evening function, or a breakfast at 7 o'clock. You do your best, but not all those things are possible, especially when you have a family. I think we can learn from men how to network — they do it during working hours. I wish I had given myself permission to do it that way, early in my career.

**Cathy Doherty**

**SVP and Group Executive, Clinical Franchise Solutions | Quest Diagnostics**

# Final Thoughts

Over the last few years, as our participants have gathered and asked questions of one another, there is one question that gets asked frequently to the women in senior management roles.

## Is it worth it?

I think Sue Liddie, Group VP and CIO of Avon Products sums it up well...

**"Everyone, no matter at what point they are in their career and their life, must ask, 'Is this worth it?' This is such a deeply personal question. Personally, I don't feel like I have sacrificed. I have made choices. It's all in the lens you are using to look at the opportunity in front of you.**

"At the end of the day, if you're having a blast doing it, it's worth it."

Sue embodies the main theme of this book —

### Leadership AND Life.

The AND is emphasized because, for Wisdom Warriors, leadership can't work without the Living part of Life.

Stories are more interesting when you dare to try new things. They are real when they come from the heart. Getting underneath the lessons, working through the hard stuff, sharing vulnerabilities with each other — that's where it really makes a difference. To grow, we need to share our experiences.

So close the book **AND......**

## GO, DO, *and* BE *a* wisdom warrior.

Thank you

C

# Gratitudes

You can't write a book without a good subject and great content. I am grateful to so many who have been instrumental in bringing this book to life.

My gratitude goes to **Roger Fransecky**. Though you are not here to see *Wisdom Warriors* come to life, I know you are smiling on all of us for sharing the wisdom you encouraged us to pass along.

To all of the **Signature Program** and **Signature Select graduates** — your continued enthusiasm and persistence in staying true to yourselves invigorated me to get the wisdom in writing so we can pass it along. As of the writing of this book, 400 amazing women have provided inspiration to, and support within, the network. *I have learned so much.*

To our **devoted faculty** — you make a difference in so many lives each time you facilitate part of the program: *Patti Milligan, Kristi Hedges, Kari Groh, Heidi Gardner, Tracy Spears, Ronee Hagen, Ann Fandozzi, Andrea Saia,* and *Genevieve Bos.*

To our **panelists** — you unselfishly share your vulnerabilities and hard-earned experiences. Those not already listed as contributors in the book include: *John Brock* and *Sol Daurella* of *Coca-Cola European Partners, Beth Axelrod, formerly with eBay, Steve Vorhees* and *Bob Beckler* of *WestRock, Wenda Harris Millard* of *MediaLink, Charlie Whitacre* of *Altria Group, David Sims* of *Perrott Knoll Limited, Eva Sage-Gavin* of *Skills for America's Future, Jeff Semenchuk* and *Rena Reiss* of *Hyatt Hotels, Joe Eckroth* of *TE Connectivity, Kath Barrow* of *EY, Kim Armor* of *Comcast NBCUniversal, Lynn Minella* of *BAE Systems, May Ngai Seeman* of *MEAG-NY, Mike Zimmer* of *Xerox, Ola Arvidsson* of *Arla Foods, Pamela Carlton* of *Springboard, Philippe Vivien* of *Alixio, Steve Milovich* of *The Walt Disney Company,* and *Valarie Gelb* of *the BarnYard Group.*

You can't write a book alone. Thank you to the instrumental team that made this all come together.

To **Rob** and **Michelle Seymour** — your constant encouragement and ability to push me beyond my perceived capabilities, along with your whiteboarding, restructuring, project management, editing, proofreading, and design ideas, have made this book a reality. Thank you for making me stick to my guns (and my voice) so that I didn't compromise.

To **Sarah Davis** — you are the "key grip" at Signature Leaders. You make everything work with a positive heart and smile. Thank you from the bottom of my heart for being the best angel on my shoulders.

To *Ilyce Glink, Kris Mackenzie,* and *Angus Carroll* of Think Glink Media — you provided the best ongoing advice and production management anyone could ask for. Your constant encouragement, eye for detail, and passion for creating a beautiful book we can all be proud of shines through.

To *Patti Frey* — *no one* can hold a candle to your ability to bring design mastery to life (as well as your ability to wordsmith, negotiate word counts, and text editing). Add your patience AND ease to work with … hands down, you are the best GIFT to us. You have been a joy, and alas, the perfect high note to end this song. I might even do another book with you around!

To our Web Design team — thank you, *Rachelle Kuramoto,* for your outstanding marketing ideas and project management; *Abby Pickus,* for your amazing design work on our website and lotus symbol for Signature Leaders; and *Marc Parry*, for your precision and speed on development.

To *Heather McClain* — your copyediting is persistent, consistent and flexible. Thank you!

To *Gianna Galle* — you have been a great partner for social media strategy and execution. Thank you for holding my hand and showing me this was the way I needed to go.

To *Kellie Ann Myrtle* — your infographics add the extra "pop" we were looking for. Thank you for your creativity and speed!

**You can't write a book without inspiration.**

To *Paige Seymour* — your constant encouragement, and ability to make me step back and reflect, always keeps me centered and grateful for the blessings I receive each day. Thank you for opening my heart to experience life's gifts.

To my leadership role models throughout my career — *Peter Bogan*, my first boss at *Mead Paperboard* when I started my career; *Carter Smith*, President of *Mead Coated Board*, who included me in VP meetings when I was a mere pup on the leadership ladder; *Dave Crow at Accenture,* for the immense support of the "outsider" to the organization; *Peter Bourke*, who included me in his circle of influence, and later hired me to lead some amazing initiatives when he was President of *Spherion*; and *Rick Smith*, for hiring me in as "Lucky #7" employee at *World50*, and giving me the green light to create, grow, and build a unique network company that became one of the best assets in the marketplace (and for my future).

**You can't write a book without support.**

To my posse — for always being there and guiding me to stay true to my authentic self … even when I am not that much fun to be around. Hugs to *Cynthia McCague*, *LeighAnne Baker*, *Jane Leipold*, *Marcia Avedon, Linda Maclean, Jodi Moore, Jean Holloway, Lou Reavis, Delynna Marshburn, Linda Homyak, Mischel Pendleton, Tina Tromiczak, Lisa Butler, Elsa Amouzgar, Anda Cristescu, Leslie Pchola, Lark Will, Heather Milligan, Bonnie Foxworth, Chris Munro, Bret Bero, Steve Hilton, Lucien Alziari, Sandy Ogg,* and *Pete Paoli.*

To the "foundation team" during start-up mode of Signature — *Miriam Jameson, Johanna Zeilstra, Dede Bell,* and *Stephanie Edwards*. Each of you added your own ideas during the journey to make Signature better and better. Thank you.

To **Charles Calhoun** — for more than 10 years, you have had an unbelievable ability to see around the corner ahead of me … and you were the one who told me it was my obligation to do this book for others. I am grateful for you.

To **Kenny Wall** — you always know the perfect time to make me take "deep breaths" and recalibrate life AND work. You have no idea how much I value you.

To **Jay Cohen** — the financial guru who provides great expertise on investments and future planning, but is the friend who peels back the layers to understand what is personally important to me.

To **Shephard King** — you have been a wonderful accountability partner. You provided the ongoing encouragement for both my mental state during writing the book and for my physical stamina, as you ensured I stuck to my workout plan. You always ask the right questions, provide the positive daily dose of encouragement, and you are a great delivery man for much needed food when my refrigerator is bare.

To **Laurie Amerson** — though I've known you for just 3 years, you fill a lifetime of friendship. Thanks for believing in me when I fail to believe in myself. **You are the best.**

# Significance of The Lotus

The Lotus Flower is the symbol we chose for Signature Leaders. It is a symbol with rich meaning in many cultures and religions, including ancient Egyptian culture, Hinduism, and Buddhism. For Buddhists, the lotus represents purity and spiritual enlightenment as it blooms through the murky waters. But each lotus of a different color represents a different aspect of life, from wisdom and knowledge to self-awakening to love and compassion. Our lotus symbol uses a multi-color graphic with a continuous line weaving among the petals to demonstrate that we evolve over time and across many different dimensions. Each lotus flower is unique and beautiful just as stories are in this book — they touch on all aspects of Leadership AND Life.

*Wisdom Warriors* are lotus flowers in full bloom.

# Notes

**Introduction:**

1. To learn more about World50, visit www.world50.com (pg. ix)

**Chapter One: Authenticity**

1. Stanley, Andy. "THE LAND OF ER Part 1 of 3," YouTube videos, 42:10, September 14, 2014, *https://www.youtube.com/watch?v=ClcrGZ0OqZo*. (pg. 6)

2. Goff, Bob. *Love Does*. Nashville: Thomas Nelson, 2012. (pg.7)

3. Blanding, Michael, "Excellence Comes from Saying No," *Harvard Business School Working Knowledge*. June 17, 2015. Accessed July 7, 2016. http://hbswk.hbs.edu/item/excellence-comes-from-saying-no. (pg. 7)

4. Hedges, Kristi. *The Power of Presence: Unlock Your Potential to Influence and Engage Others*. New York: AMACOM, 2012. (pg. 13)

**Chapter Two: Power**

1. Kay, Katty and Claire Shipman, *The Confidence Code: The Science and Art of Self-Assurance – What Women Should Know*, New York: HarperCollins Publishers, 2014. (pg. 50)

2. Barsh, Joanna, and Lareina Yee. "Unlocking the full potential of women at work." McKinsey & Co. 2012. http://www.mckinsey.com/business-functions/organization/our-insights/unlocking-the-full-potential-of-women-at-work. (pg. 54)

3. Azinger, Paul and Dr. Ron Braund. *Cracking the Code: The Winning Ryder Cup Strategy: Make it Work for You*, Decatur, GA: Looking Glass Books, 2010. (pg. 54)

4. Lencioni, Patrick M. *The Five Dysfunctions of a Team: A Leadership Fable*, San Francisco: Jossey-Bass, 2002. (pg. 65)

**Chapter Three: Peace**

1. Scott Peltin is the CEO and Co-founder of Tignum and our partner since the inception of The Signature Program. To learn more about the work that Tignum does, visit www.tignum.com. (pg. 98)

2. Peltin, Scott and Jogi Rippel. *Sink, Float or Swim, Sustainable High Performance Doesn't Happen by Chance – It Happens by Choice*, Munich: Redline Verlag, 2009. (pg. 98)

3. Peter Koestenbaum, Ph.D., is the founder and Chairman of PiB and the Koestenbaum Institute. To learn more about Peter Koestenbaum's work, visit http://www.pib.net/model.htm (pg. 100)

4. Vanderkam, Laura. *I Know How She Does It: How Successful Women Make the Most of Their Time*, New York: Penguin Group, 2015. (pg. 104)

5. Gregory Thomas, Susan. *How to Make Time for Yourself*. More Magazine, November, 2015. (pg. 105)

6. Brown, Stuart. *Play: How it Shapes the Brain, Opens the Imagination, and Invigorates the Soul*. New York: Penguin Group, 2009. (pg. 122)

7. Wadors, Pat. "I'm an introverted executive in Silicon Valley – how the heck did that happen?!" *Pulse-LinkedIn*, August 27, 2014, https://www.linkedin.com/pulse/20140827184904-4435217-i-m-an-introverted-executive-in-silicon-valley-how-the-heck-did-that-happen. (pg. 123)

8. Leider, Richard J. and David A. Shapiro. *Repacking Your Bags: Lighten Your Load for the Rest of Your Life*. San Francisco: Berrett-Koehler Publishers, Inc., 2012. (pg. 126)

**Chapter Four: Relationships**

1. Waldinger, Robert. "Robert Waldinger: What makes a good life? Lessons from the longest study on happiness." Lecture, TEDxBeaconStreet, Boston, MA, November, 2015. (pg. 133)

2. Rob Cross is an associate professor at the McIntire School of Business, University of Virginia. Rob has published numerous articles and studies, many with the Harvard Business Review and is also co-author of the book, *The Hidden Power of Social Networks*. (pg. 138)

3. Dulworth, Michael. *The Connect Effect: Building Strong Personal, Professional, and Virtual Networks*. San Francisco: Berrett-Koehler Publishers, Inc., 2008. (pg. 166)

# Index

## Q&As with Wisdom Warriors

be true to yourself